Longears,
the Moon
& Artichokes

Longears, the Moon & Artichokes
Published October, 2006
by Lulu.com

All rights reserved
Copyright 2006 by Charles F. Gill
Cover and book design by Charles F Gill
charles.gill@comcast.net

ISBN 978-0-6151-3529-8

Manufactured in the United States of America

Thanks to Elaine LeMasters

To Dad

Contents

Introduction

Artichoke. The word artichoke is taken from the Arabic أرضي شوكي (ardi shauk), meaning literally, "ground-thorn". The Globe artichoke (*Cynara cardunculus* var. *scolymus* L.) is a species of thistle. The edible part of the plant is the base (receptacle) of the artichoke head in bud, properly called a vegetable as it is harvested well before any fruit develops.

Dioscorides refers to its cultivation on a large scale near Great Carthage. Today, the Globe Artichoke is cultivated mainly in France, Italy, and Spain. In the United States, California provides nearly one hundred percent of the local crop, and approximately eighty percent of that is grown in Monterey County. Castroville in Monterey County proclaims itself "The Artichoke Center of the World" (a claim with no basis in international reality). In 1949, Marilyn Monroe was crowned the first official California Artichoke Queen in Castroville.

Artichokes are a marine climate vegetable and thrive in the cooler coastal climates. Freezing temperatures will kill the buds and hot, dry conditions destroy the tenderness, however, artichokes do like full sun. Globe Artichokes are perennials and produce the edible flower only during the second and subsequent year. The peak season for artichoke harvesting is the spring, but they continue to be harvested throughout the summer, with another peak period in mid-autumn.

Pliny speaks of their medicinal virtues. They are a good source of potassium—one large artichoke contains twenty-five percent of the RDA for folacin. The calorie content of artichokes varies according to size and length of storage. A large artichoke contains approximately fifty-eight calories. A single medium artichoke has about six grams of carbohydrates.

Ears. The pinna (Latin for feather) is the visible part of the ear that resides outside of the head. Also called the auricle, it is often used for hanging earrings and resting eyeglasses, pencils, and cigarettes; but its primary purpose is to collect sound. It acts as a funnel and amplifies the sound, directing it into the ear canal. The pinna also serves as filtering processor, adding directional information to the sound.

There are several visible ear abnormalities:

- · Bat ear—an ear that sticks out or protrudes
- · Cryptotia—hidden ear
- · Cup deformity—helical rim is compressed
- · Darwinian tubercle—a projection from the helical rim
- · Lop ear—the top ear folded over
- · Macrotia—small ears
- · Rim kinks
- · Stahl's bar—Spock ear (pointed at the top)

Ear surgery, or otoplasty, is usually done to set prominent ears back closer to the head or to reduce the size of large ears. For the most part, the operation is done on children between the ages of four and fourteen. Ears are almost fully grown by the age four, and the earlier the surgery, the less teasing and ridicule the child will have to endure. Ear surgery on adults is also possible, and there are generally no additional risks associated with ear surgery on an older patient.

Most surgeons recommend that parents stay alert to their child's feelings about protruding ears; don't insist on the surgery until your child wants the change. Children who feel uncomfortable about their ears and want the surgery are generally more cooperative during the process and happier with the outcome.

Dumbo, an anthropomorphic elephant was ridiculed for his big ears, but it turned out that he was capable of flying by using them as wings. His big ears didn't just get him off the ground—they stopped him from overheating, say researchers. Their study of heat loss from the elephant shows that his cooling system was so efficient he would have died of hypothermia if he had rested for too long.

Moon. Called Luna by the Romans, Selene and Artemis by the Greeks. Although the Moon keeps the same side towards Earth, careful observations will reveal one can actually see fifty-nine percent of the Moon's surface. These variations are caused by the fact that the Moon rotates at a constant rate, but travels around Earth at a variable rate, being in an elliptical orbit and moving faster when it is closer. Ancient observers of the moon believed that the dark regions on its face were oceans, giving rise to the Latin name "mare" (sea), which is still used today.

Many cultures around the world, including Tibet, China, Africa, Ceylon, and some Native Americans, said that a hare lived on the Moon along with the ruling Moon deity.

In India, Chandras, the god of the moon, carries a hare (sasa), hence the moon is called Sasanka, meaning "hare mark" or "spot". In Sanskrit, the moon is called Sasanka, which also means, "having the marks of a hare".

Representations of a hare or rabbit on the moon are found in the art of ancient China and in Pre-Columbian Mexico. Mythologies of both areas also place a rabbit on the moon. Although such linkage might appear to be arbitrary, a comparison of the visible surface of the full moon with the silhouette of a rabbit does reveal a degree of congruence. Not only have the distinctive ears of the rabbit, but also other features appeared to be delineated on the moon's surface.

Steve and Sirius were sitting seriously on the slippery roof pounding nails into the heavy shake shingles when the purple Pontiac pulled into the parking lot. Steve didn't recognize the middle-aged man manning the steering wheel, but there was no mistaking the attractive young passenger. It was Trudy Mills, his former on and off girlfriend from Indiana. Sirius continued pounding seriously, and the racket caused her to look up as she was climbing out of the car. Upon seeing and recognizing Steve, she called up to him. The surprise and resulting distraction caused Steve to miss the nail he was pounding, and he hit his thumb. While shaking his wounded double-phalange digit he didn't know what to do other than to respond, "Hello, Trudy, what brings you to Big Sur? Hold on, I'll be right down."

Steve reached for the umbrella that he maintained up on the rooftop held in place in a nail keg. While holding Ella's umber shade he then walked to the edge of Adam's eaves and jumped. As he glided down holding the sunshade like Marty Pippins, he was able to maneuver it such that he landed gracefully in front of Trudy and her associate, missing his foot by only inches.

"Hello, Trooty, what brings you to Big Slur?" He spoke while folding his umbrella and brushing the paint from his eLvis.

"I'm on my way to Santa Barbera. I have a cousin who's getting married. I want you to meet my fiancé. Steve, this is Fred Saladburger; Fred this is Steve Franks. Steve and I had a fickle friendship a long time ago."

A long time ago? I don't think so. Steve thought to himself. *It was more like only a couple eons ago. I suppose that would qualify as a long time ego.*

Steve had met Trudy while he was in high school. He was a junior at Richburg High and she was a freshman at Marston, the county's seat. For a long time Marston was only twice the size of Richburg and had many things Richburg didn't have such as a this, a that and a whatever, but then the Honda

Plant opened in Marston and the town morphed into a city overnight. Richburg used to have much more going on, but after the shopping malls and Wal-Mart opened in nearby Delaware, the small stores and shops such as Noman's Meat Market, the Better Baker Buns and Livingston's Depart Depot slowly disappeared two by four. What remained was a wide empty street lined with vacant opportunities with either 'for sale' or 'for lease' signs in most of the windows.

To many who had lived there for a long time it all happened gradually. Unaware that each trip to Delaware meant another nail in the proverbial coffin for the small town, they scarcely noticed that it had taken on the look of a deserted ghost town.

Steve started this small musical group called the 'Blue Bird Serenaders' and was looking for a gig—a place to play— and he found it in nearby Marston. Once about every other weekend he was able to line up either a school dance or a party at someone's house. These were never financial opportunities. These performances endured strictly for the love of the art or the attention that it brought to him, not necessarily in that order.

It was at one such school dance that Steve saw Trudy. She was pretty and neat and wore her hair piled high on her head with a blue bow. She spent the evening with a friend seated near the dais. He noticed that she was continuously watching him, even when she was dancing, so when he was finished for the night he approached her and invited her out for coffee.

California Highway One

In Japanese tradition, rabbits live on the Moon where they make mochi - the popular snack of mashed sticky rice.

Richburg was one of those Midwestern, comfortable, easy chair WASP towns, no blacks, no Jews, nary a Catholic, just pure wholegrain wheat and soybean American. At least that is how he viewed his town before leaving home for college. He did have a Spanish teacher in high school that was Jewish— only lasted a couple years or so and left town, never spoken of again, never became a part of the community. When his dad discovered that he was sharing a room in college with an Italian, a foreigner he called him, and Catholic no less, he threatened to pull him out of school. His wise mother thankfully put a stop to that.

It was a farming community of churches, haymows, Sears catalogues, peanut butter and jelly sandwiches, lace curtains and bib overalls. It was plain vanilla, goldilocks, and so was he. He was never destined to be a rocket scientist or a ditch digger. He knew the name of the President of the United States, but not the President of Mexico or the Prime Minister of Canada. (He wasn't aware that Mexico had a president or Canada, a prime minister.) He had a newspaper route, played on the high school football team and seemed to get along well with almost everyone, friends and adults alike. He usually wore Levi jeans and a flattop haircut and zipped around town on his 125 cc, two-cycle Harley Davidson motorcycle.

In his early years of development, Steve seemed to be a year or two behind his peers, physically, intellectually and emotionally. Facial hair took even longer to appear. When he turned sixteen and got his learner's permit to drive a car, it was as if the state had just licensed a fourteen-year old. If it is true that teenage girls develop about two years ahead of boys, then there was a four-year gap between Steve and the girls that he was dating.

After graduating from high school, he somehow managed acceptance at Indiana State University, enrolled in the ROTC program and received a commission as a butter bar second lieutenant in the US Army. Steve may have been complacent in his early years, but he wasn't stupid and by the time he had graduated from college, he had completed the rudiments of a liberal arts education. Nevertheless, the world scene hadn't yet directly impinged on his manner of life and so that explains why he registered as a republican without any warm feelings for either party.

When President Bush declared war on terror, Steve suddenly took an interest. Once he arrived in the war zone, in Baghdad, he was quick to notice the complexity of the situation, and he began reading the local rag, *Stars and Stripes*. He wanted to believe that he was serving the best interest of the US by fighting the war on terror. His belief seemed to be confirmed when the statue of Saddam Hussein was toppled, but then it began to appear that, like Humpty Dumpty, the kings' horses and the kings' men weren't going to be able to easily put Iraq together again. Near the end of his tour, the jeep that he was riding in ran over an improvised exploding devise, earning him a purple heart and a return ticket home to Walter Reed Hospital in Washington, DC.

Several months later, fully recovered from his broken arm and two broken ribs, Steven Benet Franks drove out the front gate of Fort Ord, California, with his discharge papers in hand, without fanfare, band playing or a parade in his honor, and headed off down the Coastal Highway in an older model Ford pickup truck ready to seek his fortune. His father, whom he hadn't seen in several years was living in a trailer among the rattlesnakes and cactuses in the Sonoran Desert in southern California, near Cathedral City, and this would be as good a time as any to go visit.

Today was a significant landmark in his life's timeline: graduation day, the day when he was no longer under the thumb of his parents, teachers, or the military. He was now on his own, free at last.

With a tank full of gas and a sensation of anticipation Steve headed south, past Carmel, on Highway 1, California's most scenic highway. The winding two-lane road clung snugly to the edge of the rugged cliffs overlooking the clear blue waters of the Pacific Ocean. There wasn't much traffic on the road, so he was able to both regard the view and drive at the same time. The waves below pounded violently against the rocky embankments as the frothy surf scattered green kelp and smaller trophies from the sea along the sandy beach. He imagined there were sea lions, otters and other marine life playing in the coves below. For a moment, he thought that he could see the Hawaiian Islands, or maybe even Japan, somewhere far off in the distance.

A sparkling display of bright iridescent cranberry and yellow ice plant covered most of the ground from the road to the edge of the cliffs. On the left side of the highway, the brown hillside crawled up the mountain range dotted with redwood, tan oak, madroñe, and chaparral. The large, creamy white, silken plumes of pampas grass waving high in the air on their long slender stocks meant that you could be sure that the fall season was here or, at least, wasn't far away.

It was a fried egg sunny-side up day and Steve pulled off his shirt while he eased down the highway with both windows open. The radio blasted soft rock sounds from KWAV in Monterey until the reception began to fade. He then slipped a compact disc of G Love & Special Sauce into the player, forwarded it to his favorite cut, 'Rodeo Clowns', and began to sing along while tapping the rhythm on the steering wheel as he drove. He missed playing alto saxophone in his old rock-a-billy band back in Indiana, and he hoped that the day would come when he could play again.

He reached down and pulled a can of Coke from the six-pack on the floor on the passenger side. It tasted good and he downed it quickly and reached for a second. The road was becoming increasingly narrow, and he had to apply pressure on his brakes more frequently as he headed into each oncoming curve. He could hear the squeal of his tires at each bend as he stepped on the gas halfway through each curve.

The afternoon continued and he began looking for a spot where he might pull off the road, park his truck and set up his small pup tent on the beach for the night. He had a bag of groceries in the back of his truck containing several cans of pinto beans, hot dogs and buns and a small sack of charcoal. He had never slept on the beach before, so he was eager to find the place, and moment, to unroll his sleeping bag and enjoy the sounds of the surf. Back at Fort Ord, he had been told that it was illegal to camp on the beach except at a state park. However, these recreational areas were usually full, and reservations were required months in advance. He hoped that he could find a place where he might hide his truck, slip down the cliffs, and remain out of sight from the highway. However, there were fewer trees along the way than he had imagined, and he was having a tough time discovering such a clandestine setting.

Then, without warning, a slate gray curtain of fog began to set in, hiding the mackerel sky, a sky dappled with rows of small white fleecy clouds, like the pattern on a mackerel's back. Within a few minutes, Steve could barely see the highway.

The needle on his speedometer moved slowly downward, reflecting the difficult time that he was having slicing his way through the thick damp haze. The sun, barely hanging on by the end of its fingertips, finally let go of its frail grasp, slipped, and sizzled into the distant brine. The atmosphere flowing into the darkened interior of his truck began to freshen, and he sensed from it that it was about to rain.

The mixture of darkness, fog and weak headlight beams combined to form a grainy, black and white washed-out view of the road ahead and limited his visibility to only a few feet. Slowly creeping his way forward he felt a sudden thump as his right front tire ran over something on the pavement. A horrifying sensation took hold as it occurred to him that he might have hit a dog, someone's pet. Without further reflection, he robotically applied the brakes and pulled over. Reaching into his glove box, he withdrew a small flashlight and jumped out to see what he had hit.

He began walking back in the direction of where he had felt the thump, scanning the beam from his flashlight back and forth across the pavement. It was a lonely stretch of road. There were no cars coming from either direction, but who could tell with so much fog? After walking twenty-five or thirty feet, he still was unable to find anything. A faintly noticeable cool breeze brushed past his face, arms and chest while light droplets of rain began to trickle downward visible only in the beam of his light, producing a chill on his shirtless body. He was about to give up and return to the pickup when he heard a muffled scream a few feet off to the side of the road. Slowly he walked over to where he heard the crying while redirecting the beam of his light.

It was a small rabbit lying off the berm, and it was still alive. As he approached the little bunny, it began giving off a shrill scream, which grew more anxious as he attempted to examine it. The rabbit seemed to have a broken leg, but otherwise was OK. In the ray of his light, it appeared rather tiny, perhaps only a foot long, with wet, muddy, multicolored fur, mostly brown and white with a white cottontail.

He carefully reached down and picked it up speaking softly hoping to comfort it while it squirmed and fought to free itself from his grasp. "There, there, little bunny," he whispered. "Everything will be all right. I'm going to take care of you if you'll just give me a chance." The bunny continued to squirm as Steve held it firmly in his arms and stroked it gently, its head, its ears and its back.

On the way back to the truck, the bunny felt warm snuggled against his bare chest. A car loomed from the rear and startled him just as he was trying to dodge a mud puddle. He slipped almost falling down with one arm clutching the rabbit and the other extended while catching his balance. After regaining his composure, he approached the passenger side of the truck as a second car drew near from the opposite direction. The door handle was missing, so he reached in through the open window and lifted the latch. He then placed the bunny onto the passenger seat and climbed in the driver's side. After sitting there for a few minutes he started the engine, applied the clutch then released it without putting the truck into gear. Looking down at the rabbit he smiled and spoke, "Yes sir, little rabbit; I've got the perfect name for you: Trudy."

Unable to comprehend what was happening, Trudy remained motionless, except for the constant wiggle in her nose.

Steve had had a rabbit one time before. One summer when he had been cutting hay on his father's farm, his cutter bar hit a nest of young rabbits, and one had survived. He took it back to the house and built a small cage out of some wood and chicken wire that he found in the garage. His father kept

[17]

chicken wire at home in order to wrap around the trunks of some peach trees, to keep the rabbits from chewing the bark. He had nursed the rabbit for one or two weeks and then one morning it was gone.

There was an opening in the cage, which looked as if something or someone had torn the chicken wire loose from the wooden frame. Since there was no evidence of a struggle, he always suspected that his dad had had a hand in it, but he couldn't bring himself around to making an accusation.

Finally, Steve placed his truck into gear. As he pulled away, the light droplets began to change to a heavy rain. He stopped a second time, long enough to pull a tarpaulin over the bed of his truck where he had his groceries and camping gear exposed to the elements. He quickly returned to the inside of his cab safe from the oncoming deluge.

He felt tired, and his visibility became so limited that he didn't want to continue. His euphoria suddenly flew out the window before he could crank it closed. The windshield began to fog, further limiting his vision. The wiper blades hadn't been changed for some time, and the late summer sun had rendered them dry resulting in a back and forth scratching sound. He reached for his shirt and used it as a towel, wiping away the misty haze from the windshield. He resisted putting it back on imagining that he might need it again.

He was now traveling much slower, groping along the dark wet way wishing that the rain would somehow ease, at least until he could find a place to stop for the night. He had given up the notion of camping on the beach and resigned himself to sleeping in the cab of his pickup.

Suddenly the road seemed to disappear. Thinking he had driven off it somehow, he feared that he might go off the edge. He knew the danger of slamming the brakes on slippery pavement, but he had no choice. The truck began to spin and slide off the asphalt stopping only after it had slammed against the rocky embankment on the opposite side.

Trudy had fallen to the floor and resumed her screams. He picked her up, held her, and tried to reassure her that everything was all right. The screams turned to grunts, and then eventually she settled down to nose wiggles interspersed with occasional groans.

Unable to continue farther, he stepped outside the truck and was able to see that he had plowed into a rockslide. The highway cut into the hillside, exposing it to erosion. The incessant rain had caused flooding and land movement. Heavy surf advisory was in effect for more than three hundred miles of coastline, from San Luis Obispo County to the Mexico border, with waves as high as twenty feet. The road closure had stranded him there, and unfortunately, this stretch of main thoroughfare out in the boondocks was a low priority with the Caltrans road maintenance crew.

He backed his truck safely away from the loose pile of rocks, closed his eyes and fell asleep. The rabbit remained quiet in the seat beside him.

Eventually the bulldozer crew from Caltrans arrived and worked through the night clearing the roadway.

Hours later, daylight sneaked unnoticed into the morning fog and wrapped itself around the mountains and Steven's pickup truck. He awakened with a chill, shivering from the early morning coolness, climbed out and stepped around to the ocean side of the parked vehicle to take a piss. Steam rose as the yellow stream splashed into the cool air and mixed into the sandy ground, forming a path running downhill, and then disappearing into the earth.

A few feet away he spotted some miner's lettuce. Steve gathered a handful and returned to the truck carefully placing it on the seat next to Trudy. The wounded rabbit quickly began to nibble at the green material, its wet nose moving to the rhythm of its mastication.

With his hands in his rear pockets, Steve wandered over to the edge of the cliff and looked out over the spectacular vista, the sensational meeting of land and water, and decided to climb down the rocks for a quick survey of the beach. The strong aroma of the shore filled his nostrils while the morning mist gently settled onto his face.

In the rocks and tide pools there were sea anemones and barnacles, and he spotted an occasional starfish. Stepping onto the sandy beach, he walked near the water's edge, but an incoming wave sent him scurrying backwards to avoid getting his shoes wet. A dead sea lion caught his attention, and he wandered over to look. It had been there for a while, evidenced by the large chunks of leathery skin that were missing. Strings of kelp partially covered some of the cadaver. Sand crabs scavenged in the sun-dried kelp and buried in the sand, using their antennae to rake food particles to their mouths. Kelp flies, wrack flies, rove beetles, tiger beetles, and dune beetles reamed the beach foreshore. Steven suddenly remembered that he hadn't eaten and quickly decided to return to the truck to look for a place to eat.

Continuing down the Pacific Coast Highway, they arrived at Bixby Bridge where he noticed nearby the Crocodile's Tail Restaurant. (Bixby Bridge is the crowning jewel of the Big Sur Highway and has been photographed and used in movies and television commercials. It is one the most photographed man made structures on the West Coast. At its completion, it was one of the largest single-arch concrete bridges in the world.) Unfortunately, it was still too early in the morning, and the restaurant hadn't yet opened. Steven and Trudy continued down the road with hopes of having better luck at Big Sur.

Farther on, they arrived at the Big Sur Deli just as the fog was leaving. Steven parked the truck by the front door, not too far from the small nearby Post Office. Leaving Trudy on the seat, he climbed out and made a dash for the covered porch. As he stepped up onto the gray cedar landing, he smelled the freshly brewed coffee. Opening the door, he tripped the ring-a-ding bell and entered the small coffee shop.

Moon, a young girl wearing rings on each of her fingers with long sandy brown hair draped over her beaded paisley print caftan, warmly greeted him. "Good morning. How are you today?"

"I sure am glad you're open this early. My rabbit and I haven't eaten since yesterday noontime. Can you fix me a hamburger?" He stood there with one hand in a rear pocket.

"Of course, but it is quite early in the morning." Smiling and wondering about the rabbit she continued, "Could I perhaps interest you in our nine-grain pancakes with strawberries or a wood-fired bacon and egg pizza? On the other hand, how about an avocado, bacon and cheese omelet?"

"Actually, I think I'll just have a couple of those cheese Danish there on the counter and quart of milk; and a carrot. I think I'll have my breakfast in the back, on the veranda. Do you mind if I bring my rabbit?" His other hand now rested in the remaining rear pocket.

"No, not at all. Go right ahead and I'll bring everything out to you."

Steve returned to the truck, fetched the rabbit and took a seat at one of the tables on the terrace. He placed the rabbit on the chair next to him. Moon soon arrived with his coffee and excitedly saw the furry creature shaking on the seat. "Oh! It's so cute. Can I hold it?"

"She's got a broken leg. I ran over her last night in the fog. Have you any ideas what I can do for her?"

"The poor thing; she's shaking. I can get her a towel. I'll be right back."

Moon returned with the rest of his breakfast and a towel, which she carefully used to cover Trudy. Without asking, she pulled up a chair across the table from Steve, next to the rabbit. "Say, I've got an idea. I know this person, at Cal Poly; he's a veterinary student. I should give him a call and see if he can help you. I bet that he can. I took my dog Toto to him last fall; he had a broken leg, just like Trudy, here. I bet he can fix her right up, good as new. Say, I don't know your name; mine's Moon Light. I know; it's a hippie name. My parents were hippies, so I guess that makes me one, too. My mother calls herself Starr, and they named my older brother Sirius. Can you believe it? They named him Sirius because it's the brightest star in the sky. Do you mind if I ask you your name?"

With a mouthful of Danish, he slowly finished chewing, swallowed and answered, "Steve, Steven Benet Franks. If you could call your friend, I'd really appreciate it. I'm going nowhere in particular, maybe to Palm Desert. I'll probably be in San Luis Obispo later this afternoon, and I could meet him there, if that's alright?"

"You're from Fort Ord, aren't you? I can tell, the short hair and all. That isn't a problem. Anyone who cares for a broken rabbit has to be OK in my book. Do you have any brothers and sisters? Oh my, I'm getting too personal, aren't I?"

"I don't mind. Yes, I have a brother in Denver. He's in the oil business, got a wife and a kid, you know the story. I'm just not ready for that. No sisters, though."

For the next few minutes they talked together, both forgetting the time when a tall young man donning an Afro, a tie-dyed T-shirt and huaraches, wiping his hands with a hand towel stepped down onto the veranda and informed Moon that there were other customers inside that were waiting for her. Without stopping for a reaction, he returned inside, and Moon quickly got up from her chair, a bit embarrassed, and backed away from the table. "That's my brother Sirius. We both work this deli together. I have to get inside and get to work. But hold tight, I'm going to call my friend, and I'll get right back to you."

Minutes later Moon scurried out the door and excitedly told Steve that she had talked with Jordan, her veterinarian friend, and that he would be available this afternoon around 3:00. She gave Steve a paper with his name, address and phone number as well as her own phone number. "Please call me after you've met with Jordan. I hope to see you again. You will call me, won't you?"

Steve carefully took the rabbit into his arms and exited through the deli and out the front door. On the way out, he nodded goodbye to Sirius while detecting a defiant stare.

Trudy and Steve hit the road heading south. The early fall day seemed to turn inside out as the eastern sun continued its climb over the rugged range to his left: warm and glowing, powerful and dependable, shining, cheery, life-giving. The warm breeze blew inside the truck through the open windows causing Trudy's furry coat to vibrate in irregular spasms.

Moon had made a favorable impression on him, and he scarcely noticed the passing landscape as he reviewed in his mind his encounter with her. Her attraction was immediate. Her smile, her openness to him, her down-to-earth quality all added to her magnetism. He especially noticed her long sandy hair, which was parted on top and hung down the sides of her face cascading down her shoulders and back.

Steve had had several girl friends from his time in high school and throughout college. None of them had been serious relationships. He had never been able to score sexually with any of them except for heavy kissing and petting, and on a few occasions, he had got his fingers wet. However, he hadn't had any relationship since Trudy Mills back in Indiana. He liked her a lot, but it wasn't love, he was sure of that. The last time they were together she expressed her desire to go to bed with him, but only if he would confess his love for her.

While in the army, he thought of her from time to time, considered writing to her and then dismissed the notion. About a year later, he received a letter from her stating that she was going to be in Texas, near where he was stationed, and that she would like to meet with him. He ignored the letter and didn't respond.

The trip from Big Sur took less time than Steve had imagined as the great rock at Morro Bay came into view. Once in San Luis Obispo, he took the California Boulevard exit off Highway 101, entered the campus and purchased a general-use parking permit at one of the several vending machines. From there, he made his way to the Animal Science Office and on to the student-run vet clinic, where he met Jordan Charnofsky.

"Oh yes, Moon said that you were coming. And what do we have here, a small cottontail, *sylvilagus audubonii*, I believe. Yes, we do have a nasty break. Have a seat over there. I'll fix her up and you can be on your way. By the way, how do you know Moon?"

"I only met her this morning after hitting this poor bunny on the road last night in the fog near Big Sur. There was no place near for me to take her, so when I met Moon for breakfast, I couldn't tell if she felt sorrier for me or for the rabbit. That's when she decided to call you. She said you were friends."

"Yes, we went to high school together. She's a terrific girl, woman, I mean. If you spend any time with her, you'll discover her uniqueness. She lives alone with her mother and brother, and they make a living there at the restaurant. A grizzly bear killed her father up in Canada several years ago. After that, it was too difficult for them to stay so they returned to Loma Vista where Starr's mother lived. A short while later they started this deli, which has grown into a real success story. She studied at home with her mother until she turned thirteen when she wanted to be out with others her age. She entered high school, one grade ahead of her contemporaries. In spite of her eagerness to come in to the outside world (and given that a large number of her social group were of the flower generation, seemingly open to new and strange circumstances and personalities) her ability to navigate the intricate social structure of Big Sur High proved to be more difficult than she'd imagined."

"Well, like I said, have a seat over there and I'll get started."

Several minutes later, Jordan returned with the rabbit. "It was a compound fracture, and I had to use this special splint. She'll have to wear it for some time, so you'll have to take care of her. May I ask what you plan to do with her?"

"I guess I'll just keep her with me in my pickup until it's comes time to turn her loose. I sure hope that I don't become too attached to her. Perhaps her foot will bring me good luck."

"You need to know that lagomorphs like this rarely survive. However, what can one do? Just do the best you can. That's all that you can do."

That evening, when Jordan returned home from working at the student-run vet clinic, he tried watching *Mutual of Omaha's Wild Kingdom: Black Mamba,* on the Animal Planet Network, but was unable to keep his attention on it. He felt nervous and anxious; his hands were perspiring. He knew what was eating at him; he tried sit-ups, pushups, and stretches thinking that would distract him.

He fixed himself an avocado on rye sandwich and a barley green salad and washed them down with Himalayan goji juice. He realized that he had made a foolish mistake and if he didn't act quickly, she would be gone forever. Pressing number 1 on his autodial cell phone, he waited as it rang on the other end repeatedly until a cheerful voice answered.

"Hello! Big Sur Deli."

Starr Light

Henri Luis Delgado sat on a three-legged stool in front of the river rock fireplace in his small rented cabin in the redwoods of the Santa Cruz Mountains, dumbfounded. *What is this letter from the draft board?* He quickly tossed it into the burning flames and tried to put it out of his mind. It had to be a mistake. There was no reason to be concerned over it.

The letter gracefully danced a short ballet over the rising heat of the flames before coasting to the edge of the stone hearth untouched by the blaze. He continued to sit there staring at the letter that had somehow partially submerged itself in the soft gray remains from yesterday's fire. "Burn, dammit!" he exclaimed, and he reached in to push the letter back into the flames. Then he withdrew it, shook the ashes and began to re-read.

'You are hereby directed to present yourself for Armed Forces Physical Examination to the Local Board named above by reporting at: 1000 S. Main Street, Room 107, Salinas, California 93901.'

Henri understood what this meant. President Johnson had already sent close to 500,000 troops to Viet Nam for this foolish war, and President Nixon had failed to bring any of the troops home even after it had been determined to be unwinnable.

The newspapers continued to report that Secretary of State Kissinger was beginning to see a 'light at the end of the tunnel', but the bodies of American soldiers continued to stream home in body bags.

Years earlier, the French had learned the lessons of Viet Nam the hard way too, after a hundred years of failure at colonization, ending with a total defeat of the French Expeditionary Corps at the battle of Dien Bien Phu.

Henri crumpled the letter for a second time and tossed it into the hungry flames, this time it took only a few seconds for the notice to be completely consumed.

Reaching for his guitar, he began to strum, slowly and softly. As the melody and rhythm began to develop, he increased the tempo little by little and began evoking utterances as if speaking in tongues. Music was Henri's passion. Whenever he was down, music would lift him up. Whenever he was lonely, it provided him with companionship and entertainment. It supplied him with a means of earning a living. He would never be rich, he knew that, but what he received was sufficient to pay his rent in his one-room cabin on San Lorenzo Road, halfway between Felton and Boulder Creek, and to buy food and cigarettes. He could sing and perform nearly all of the popular styles of music, but he enjoyed folk music for the most part—that way he could be creative. Without having a particularly pleasing voice, he could allow his emotions to cut loose. With folk music, he could more easily say those things that he wanted to say. Mostly, he enjoyed listening to Ramblin' Jack Elliott, Cisco Houston and Dave Van Ronk. He had heard Van Ronk perform at the Boulder Creek Theater one night and learned that the promoters had sold tickets, both in advance and at the door, and had then taken the money and left town without paying Van Ronk.

He played and sang in coffee shops and bookstores, often with his girlfriend, Starr Light, who shared his mountain cabin. She was a couple of years older than Henri, had been born and raised in Boulder Creek, had a passion for writing poetry and played the Autoharp.

Together they made a good singer songwriter team. Except for her large ears, she was very attractive, and that was good for business. Her interests were much more far-reaching. She had loved myths and fairytales as a child and had read most of the books of Joseph Campbell. She also owned several books on the tarot and was teaching herself some in depth divinatory practices such as palmistry, the reading of tealeaves, crystal ball scrying, runes and tarot.

She would frequently dress very colorfully and she was handsomely decked with flashy but inexpensive jewels. On some occasions, she would appear very happy and other times she resembled the last rose of summer. Using pictures from the Rider-Waite deck, she would describe each card in the Major Arcana from the viewpoint of 'The Fool', and his journey to reach his ultimate goal, 'The World'.

Henri said nothing about the notice to Starr. He reasoned that he could claim conscientious objector status. If he had to, he would go to Canada. After all, some of his early years had been spent living with his father in Montreal. He had attended three semesters there at McGill University, but the winters were cold. (That is why a large part of Montreal exists as an underground city, La Ville Souterraine.)

On the advice of his good friend Jerry Lathrup, he had left Montreal and come to California, the sunshine state, to be warm. This expatriate could return if he had to.

Henri and Starr had met in a coffee house/bookstore called Geno's Studio in downtown Santa Cruz. There was usually some form of entertainment each night, usually folk singers. Some evenings there would be poetry readings. The place was well known, and had a reputation for attracting such notables as Allen Ginsberg, Jack Kerouac and Tim Leary. Jerry Garcia, who lived in La Honda, and Dave Guard in Woodside would stop in from time to time. Other locals included Grace Slick, Stevie Nicks and Lindsay Buckingham.

Thursday nights were reserved for 'open mike' and anyone that wanted could come early, sign in the roster and get a turn on the small stage in the rear. It was a small venue, only fifty seats, but some evenings the place would be filled with every available spot taken by standing onlookers.

Henri had just arrived from Canada. He was an unknown performer, and his friend Jerry suggested to him that he should show up at Geno's Studio for open mike.

Before moving to Los Angeles for a job with IBM, Jerry had spent many evenings either playing or listening to the continuous flow of poets and musicians that frequented the place.

On his first night, Henri sat in the back row waiting his turn at the mike while watching the performers scheduled ahead of him. The MC introduced Starr Light, and she began to sing. Her voice was clear, and she plucked her wide-neck eight-string classical guitar with all five fingers as if she were playing a harp. She wore a long dashiki style Indian print dress and Indian buffalo sandals. Her long sandy hair draped down over her shoulders.

Henri's turn was next. He sang the song written and made famous by Johnny Cash.

At my door the leaves are falling.
A cold wild wind has come.
Sweethearts walk by together.
And I still miss someone.

Both Henri Delgado and Starr Light were the outstanding performers of the evening. When everyone that was going to perform was finished, they both returned together and sang the Sonny and Cher song, 'I Got You Babe.' The audience loved them both and applauded loudly.

[29]

After sending several notices and receiving no response from Henri, the local draft board decided to send a field rep out to meet him in person. This individual was in the form of Sergeant Andrew Hillandale, who parked his olive drab jungle camouflaged Land Rover on the side of the single lane San Lorenzo Road with the wheels on the right side of the vehicle embedded into the ditch. His uniform was smartly pressed, and his black combat boots shined as if they were made of patent leather. His cunt cap sat perched with a slight tilt on his head. On his chest, he proudly wore several tiers of ribbons, one of which was a Purple Heart, another, the Bronze Star with oak leaf cluster and the National Defense Service Medal. Above the ribbons was the blue and silver Combat Infantry Badge, which meant that he had seen combat.

After striking three sharp raps on the cabin door, he stepped back one pace, snapped to attention and awaited a response. There was no answer and he repeated the drill, a second, third and fourth time. He wasn't ready to surrender, not yet.

Stepping down from the porch, he walked around to the side of the house and peered into the window. There, Sergeant Hillandale was able to get a good perspective of his quarry's domicile. The focal point of the room was the large fireplace made of round, gray river rock that covered the wall to his right. In front of the fireplace on the floor were several throw pillows, cushions and a low-level coffee table made out of a hatch cover from a fishing boat mounted on wrought iron legs at each end. On the table, there were several empty beer bottles, an overflowing ashtray and several music books. Very near to the hatch cover was a three-legged stool with a Martin dreadnought guitar leaning against it. On the left side of the fireplace there were homemade bookshelves stacked three high mounted on two columns of concrete bricks. He could barely make out the titles of *East of Eden*, *The Moon is Down* and

On the Road. There was an overstuffed chair in one corner on the right near the wall. Over the fireplace was a framed picture of Chief Joseph of the Nez Perce Indians. On a second wall, there was a wall hanging of the 'Tree of Life'. Not too far from the hatch cover was a second round top table with a kitchen chair parked next to it holding a crystal ball and a deck of tarot cards laying face up. The top card was the fool.

Sergeant Hillandale inserted a copy of the official notice in between the door and the door jam together with a copy of his business card on which he wrote the words, 'Please call me.' He then returned to his Land Rover and pulled away, out of the ditch.

Starr arrived home that afternoon before Henri and saw the notice as she entered the cabin door. Normally calm and collected, she paced the cabin floor nervously waiting for Henri to return. When dinnertime arrived, he still hadn't appeared home and her tension began to grow. By midnight, he still hadn't returned, and she decided to do a meditation exercise.

When feeling stressed she would often do a walking meditation as the monks in monasteries used to do: walk the quadrangle. Since she didn't have a quadrangle, she walked to the rear of the cabin and took the well-worn path which led up to the top of the mountain. She took in slow deep breaths and then she let them out slowly while being conscious of her body. She felt or sensed her entire body. While walking, she mentally observed how her body was functioning without judging or criticizing it, just being aware of it. She was careful not to be rushed.

As she walked and breathed, a thought came into her head, which said, 'This is silly.' She pushed it gently away, and resumed walking. After ten or fifteen minutes, she stopped, having realized what course she was about to embark upon. She then returned to her cabin and went to bed.

In the morning she awoke and felt Henri's body spooned against her back. She hadn't heard him when he came home and had no idea when he had arrived or why he had retuned so late. She sensed that the draft notice had something to do with his strange behavior, that is, if his coming home late was to be considered as strange behavior.

Knowing that this morning was the twelfth day in her menstrual cycle she removed her panties, turned toward him and mounted. She took in slow deep breaths, and then she let them out slowly while being conscious of her body. If she were to conceive, there had to be no pressure, no stress.

She felt his warm seed enter her body and immediately she experienced the heavens open and she seemed to hear a chorus of angels singing praises to her divine nature. She saw a bright star shoot across the sky and then later, she saw a moon.

When it was over, she dismounted and rolled onto her back, careful not to lose any of his juices. As she closed her eyes, she remembered how her mother had once spoken to her of her ancestors and their belief that they were of divine origin. She could never be sure if it were true or not, but now at this moment, she wanted it to be so. The only sign given to her was her ears.

If it were to be a boy, she would call him Sirius, the brightest star in the sky; if it were to be a girl, she would call her Moon.

Henri was home playing his guitar when Sergeant Hillandale arrived one week later. This time Henri opened the door and invited him in. Henri sat on the three-legged stool and offered the overstuffed chair to Hillandale, without realizing that Hillandale had the advantage of looking down on him. The Sergeant presented the official notice and Henri explained that he would have to declare himself as a conscientious objector. Hillandale had no objection to that since it wasn't up to him. That would need to be adjudicated by the Selective Service Board. He did explain, "It is very complicated; it is not easy to establish a conscientious objector status. Not very many applications are approved.

"According to US military law, a soldier who fails to report for duty within thirty days is AWOL, with a maximum penalty of five years confinement, forfeiture of all pay and allowances, and a dishonorable discharge. After thirty days, he or she is technically a deserter. The maximum penalty for desertion in time of war is death, although no US soldier has been executed for desertion since World War II."

One week later, Henri and Starr had packed all their belongings into their 1959 VW Microbus. The only thing left behind was the overstuffed chair. They had decided together that it would be best if they moved to Vancouver, British Columbia. This way there would be no conflict. They had heard about a commune in a small out of the way community of Pender Harbor and that was to be their destination.

They drove all day and night north on Highway 101 through Redding, California; Medford, Eugene and Salem, Oregon; and Seattle, Washington to Vancouver, BC; then from Horseshoe Bay in West Vancouver via the Sunshine Coast ferry to Pender Harbor.

Jim Havilland was the son of a Hollywood movie mogul. When Jim graduated with a degree in finance from undergraduate school at UCLA, his father bought him a new Ferrari. There was an expectation on his father's part that Jim would continue on to graduate school while remaining close to his father's side in the movie industry. Jim intended to comply with his father's wishes, and why not? He was being handed the keys to a very lucrative and exciting career.

Halfway through the year, Jim fell in love with Joyce Loveless, a young girl in undergraduate school. Joyce was a member of the SDA, Students for Democratic Action, and was active in its antiwar, anti-Vietnam activities. Together they spent hours promoting protests and rallies as well as campaigning for liberal candidates to political offices both on and off campus.

Joyce could summarily be described as nearly pleasingly plain looking, sexually intoxicating, intellectually gifted, and ambitious. Jim on the other hand was quite handsome, but not as talented intellectually and certainly not motivated toward any short or long-term purpose.

As they began to spend more and more time together, Joyce moved out of her college dormitory room into Jim's plush off-campus apartment. Joyce was able to keep her grades up and remain active in her extracurricular activities; however, Jim was unable to balance more than two plates at a time. She gave him five stars for sexual performance, and that alone was enough to keep her from packing her suitcases.

At the end of the second semester, Jim concluded that the combination of graduate school, working at his father's office, attending sit-ins and protests, and nightly pumping Joyce into multiple orgasmic climaxes had only rewarded him with a university layoff notice. Jim had flunked-out. Several days later, he received his draft notice.

Jim wasn't going to be drafted, that was for sure, and he was bright enough at least to know that he could never convince a selective service board of granting him conscientious objector status. With that, he made the first significant decision ever in his twenty-two years of life: he was going to Canada. He hoped that he could persuade Joyce to go with him, but that lofty possibility, too, sat high on the shelf, next to the selective service board. He reasoned that she had too many things going for her that she wouldn't want to trade any of them for weaving blankets and weeding a potato patch in some North Country commune. When he made it known to her that he was leaving, he warned her that if she wanted to stay at the apartment, she was on her own. If she wanted, she could leave with him for British Columbia. He explained that he had heard about several communes in the Vancouver area.

Initially she opposed the notion of either of them leaving. "The chances of surviving in the snowy backwoods of Vancouver during the coldest part of the winter are probably not much better than in the hottest part of Southeast Asia," she reasoned. "With a little creative initiative you should be able to work yourself into a cushy job, in Saigon, or Vung Tao. You certainly should be able to schmooze yourself away from the infantry, at least," she thought. "As for me, I'm deeply committed in my studies here. It would take a very large carrot."

That night she couldn't sleep. She climbed over Jim without waking him, rolled out of bed, jumped into her panties and tank top lying at the side of the bed and headed into the kitchen. A glass of non-fat milk together with a peanut butter and jelly sandwich always tasted better to her at 2:00 A.M. than any other time of the day, like hot dogs tasting better at a ball game than at home. Before she had a chance to lick the surplus peanut butter from the knife, an idea exposed itself to her more boldly than the streaker that had flashed across the quad on campus a few days earlier. Dashing back into the bedroom, she shouted, "Jim! Wake up! I've got it."

"You've got what?" Not wanting an answer, he pulled the pillow over his head.

She flipped on the small table lamp at the side of the bed. "I've got it; wake up, Jim. I've got the solution to our dilemma." Speaking excitedly, she pulled his pillow away and grabbed his arm trying to turn him over. "This can be a spectacular opportunity; we can start our own commune. Come on, Jim! Sit up and listen to me. This is a great idea. We can buy some land, somewhere out of the way but well positioned and…"

"Buy some land?" he interrupted. "Where would we get the money?"

She smiled, reached for both his hands and made eye contact as she spoke, "Sell the Ferrari!"

That caught Jim's attention and he sat up, wide-awake. "I don't see any benefit in our forming a commune. It seems easier to me to just join an existing one."

"Jim, come on now; simply joining has no purpose. We would just be going for the ride. Nothing gambled, nothing gained. If you're serious about going to Canada, you had better have a plan, a way out. For you, this could be your first investment into your future as well as your first great adventure. For me, well I thought that I could spend a year writing a book about this great adventure. In addition, with your connections, your father and his friends, it might even become a movie. Can you imagine it? Maybe Peter Fonda and Dennis Hopper would star in it."

Henri and Starr drove slowly along the road from Pender Harbor leading to the old Clifford Farm that now had a sign at the end of the lane: 'Heaven's Gate, Visitors Welcomed'. Henri turned onto the lane and drove back along a muddy rain-soaked path barely wide enough for the ancient microbus. Low growing brush and tree branches rubbed against the sides of the van, making scratching sounds as it made its way bouncing and splashing mud from the deep potholes.

After the length of a football field, the lane began to curve and incline upward, wrapping around a small hill. Henry shifted down to first gear as the incline grew steeper and steeper. The low growing brush was now a thick forest, and the daylight gave way to evening and near darkness. At the top of the hill, a vast expanse opened and Henri and Starr could see the outline of a farm below, a farmhouse, two barns and a few head of livestock.

The bus coasted down the declining slope, arriving at a small parking lot and stopped. They both remained inside, sitting quietly and looking around, not knowing quite where to start or what to do. There was one other VW microbus similar to theirs except that it was painted with brilliantly colored murals with words like, 'love', 'peace', 'make love, not war'.

Henri opened the door, stepped down onto the muddy parking lot, and stretched his arms while arching his back. A man on the distant farmhouse roof stopped what he was doing, looked in the direction of the visitors and waved. Henri returned the salutation and then looked at Starr as she was climbing out of the bus. Starr looked up and saw the person waving and she too smiled and returned the greeting.

As the two of them walked toward the house, they passed several white goats and golden chickens corralled in a fenced-in area attached to a barn, stopping long enough to pet the large buck that strolled next to the fence to greet them. One small kid was standing on a bale of hay, and a second was hiding under a sheet of plywood that was leaning up against the side of the barn. Next to the bale of hay was a small lawnmower-sized John Deer tractor with a two-wheeled wagon hooked on behind it containing several more bales of hay. On the far side of the corral there was a tall windmill slowly pumping water into a water trough. A block of white salt was hanging off the outside edge of the tank. The outside siding of the house and barn was severely weathered, and one had to approach it and look closely to see any paint. The siding had been removed from one of the outside walls exposing newly replaced studs that were waiting to be recovered on both the interior and the outside.

A face suddenly appeared from inside, between the studs. "Hello there," she spoke, surprising them both. "Can I help you?"

"Oh, hello," Henri beamed. "I'm Henri Delgado and this is Starr Light. We are both from California."

Joyce crawled out between the two wooden studs, carrying a hammer. She was wearing a red bandana tied around her head, a blue plaid woolen shirt, cut-offs, heavy-duty work shoes and a carpenter's belt containing several items with which she had obviously been working. Her long sandy hair hung down from beneath her bandana not quite to her shoulders.

As she replaced the hammer into her belt, she offered her hand, smiled and addressed them. "Hi, I'm Joyce Loveless and that lumberjack on the roof, now climbing down, I see, is my friend, Jim Havilland. We're both from California too— Los Angeles. What can I do for you?"

It was Joyce's idea, that is, to have checked with the Tax Collector's Office for a list of any abandoned properties taken over by the state for unpaid taxes. Surprisingly, there was such a list, and it included the one hundred and sixty acres that they now owned. Anyone could have taken it over by simply redeeming its unpaid assessment together with interest and penalties.

Jim had sold his Ferrari while in Los Angeles, and they moved into the old rundown farmhouse. If the local building inspector had been aware of the miserable state of disrepair of this two-story 1920s vintage wooden structure, he would certainly have condemned it and not permitted any occupancy. Several acres of the property were tillable having grown wheat and soybeans during its former years, whereas the remaining wooded portion was mostly covered with virgin forest butting up to a lake. There were several types of game including rabbits, squirrels and pheasants that to Joyce's displeasure Jim was eager to hunt.

By the end of their first month they had a few carrots, lettuce, tomato plants, beans and rhubarb stocks starting to stick their heads out from the rich, black soil that had been deposited there in earlier times by the receding glaciers. They had used very little of the proceeds of the sale of the red Italian stallion and the remaining portion was safely tucked away in their checking account. A week later, they met Benjamin and Rebecca Epstein, the first of the several couples that were to follow and to join them at Heaven's Gate.

Except for the real estate, everything was share and share alike, which included the fruits of the forest and garden and all the expenses incurred by the group. Everyone was expected to contribute a reasonable amount of work toward the group's efforts. All money earned by individuals, once they became members, went into a common treasury. In return, the community assumed responsibility for meeting all individual needs for food, shelter and medical expenses.

Henri and Starr moved into the house and took one of the upstairs bedrooms adjacent to Ben and Becky. Several weeks later, Colin Voucher and Stella Worth arrived and took the remaining bedroom. From then on as new arrivals joined the group, a row of tents was erected as temporary shelter until new rooms could be added onto the old farmhouse. When the winter months brought the bitter cold and snow, the tent dwellers were forced to come inside and find space in the living room or wherever they could find any.

Henri and Starr were both able to find opportunities in town. Starr sang and played her Autoharp every other week for Sunday brunch at the Hamilton House bed and breakfast, and on Saturday mornings, she had a small booth at the Farmers' Market where she gave palm and tarot card readings. Henri joined a bluegrass band that performed usually once a week around the province. There were often special events where they sang and played together. They were a great source of entertainment at the farm, and usually after dinner, everyone would join and sing. Nevertheless, they both continued to do their share of the work in the garden, in maintaining the house and barns and milking the goats.

Some of the members were vegetarian; others were not. The group agreed that there would be no guns or weapons on the farm. The exception was that Henri would be allowed to use his 20-gauge shotgun only for community business, which was bringing fresh meat to the kitchen. They had hoped that the majority of their food would come from their garden. During the summer, a few potatoes and vegetables had been harvested and saved in the cellar, but as the cold months passed, they soon ran out of anything to eat. During the summer months, their few tomatoes never saw enough sun to turn red, and were eaten green. The carrots only grew to finger length. Fortunately, a few members had families that were able to help to a limited degree. Nevertheless, even then, those sources were dwindling as their disappointed parents were beginning to shut off the stream of support. The community of Pender Harbor was sympathetic, and was able to provide a certain amount of support to the expatriates who were paying a high price for their antiwar convictions.

In a Christmas card to her mother, Starr had enclosed a letter describing all that was happening there at the farm. She was certain that they had made the right decision in going to Canada, and that the tribulations and hardships that they were enduring were a necessary part of their life that was unfolding. She held strong her newfound beliefs that she was of divine origin, and not only would Quetzalcoatl see them through this, but he would richly reward them. She had seen the vision of Sirius and Moon and they hadn't yet been delivered.

They had become close friends with Ben and Becky. They had both graduated from Indiana State with accounting degrees, but like everyone else, they were unable to find work.

Ben played the banjo. They had a five-year-old daughter, Emily. Emily was quite prodigious, had learned to read and write at home, and was even working on learning French. One day, Emily wandered away and was never heard from again. The entire commune scoured the area and after two weeks, finally surrendered to the fact that she wouldn't be alive.

Just as ordained, Sirius was born first and then a year later so was Moon. Without any training or skills other than their music, Henri and Starr were barely able to survive. Their grains and vegetables came mostly from the commune, and then Henri fished and hunted for the rest. Their situation had become desperate. He was a draft dodger and considered a deserter. They couldn't return to the US. One summer day while in the dense forest, Henri was mauled by a grizzly bear and died. Starr returned to Boulder Creek with her son and daughter.

Heaven's Gate Commune survived in spite of the difficult times that it underwent, further evidence that patience and persistence can win over perilous times. The disappearance of young Emily followed by the death of Henri Delgado added to the group's psychological impoverishment, which led to a winter seemingly comparable to the first winter of the sea-wearied Pilgrims from the Mayflower or the winter of the Donner Party in the Sierras. Jim Haviland took a job clerking in the Vancouver Stock Exchange and Joyce Loveless wrote her first novel, which became the basis for the Alliance for Cinema Art award for best picture of the year. They both poured their profits into the commune to keep it running until they were able to secure the rights to producing and exporting medical marijuana to those certain cities in the United States that had regionally permitted the so-called marijuana clubs to exist.

Soon after her return to the Monterey Bay, Starr heard about the Esalen Institute located on twenty-seven spectacular acres of Big Sur coastline with the Santa Lucia Mountains rising sharply behind. It was described as an alternative educational center devoted to the exploration of what Aldous Huxley called the 'human potential'.

Anxiously, she managed a trip to the center, where she was introduced to its many offerings: practices such as Gestalt, massage, sensory awareness and meditation. She enrolled and received a certificate of completion in the massage and bodywork program initially. The institute became her source of alternative education and personal growth as she continued to participate in programs that included meditation, yoga, psychology, ecology, spirituality, art and music.

One day while driving from Esalen to her cabin in Boulder Creek, she passed the Post Office at Big Sur and saw a 'For Lease' sign placed on the window of a vacant shop. The whole way home and then later that night she kept thinking about that shop wondering if there might be some opportunity in it for her. She was, after all, becoming quite skilled with private palm and tarot card readings, and with her massage and bodywork customers while working out of her home.

The next morning she returned to Big Sur, signed a month-to-month rental agreement and went to work.

Her business grew and after a year, she had saved enough to put a down payment on the adjacent house and lot that had just come on the market. It seemed like a lot of money to her, but it would enable her to move from Boulder Creek nearer to Esalen and her work, as well as giving her enough space to build the deli that she had decided on. The idea of serving healthy meals rich in grains and vegetables and alternatives such as soy and tofu would differentiate her menu from that of the typical Jewish delis. She would develop unique soups, casseroles, salads and baked goods using whole grains and organic produce.

By the time Sirius and Moon were ready to start school, Starr Light had built a successful, profitable business for herself and her two children, and she had to hire extra help to keep up the place.

Starr's mother lived in Loma Vista, in the interior around Fresno County. Not everyone in the family line had the unique ears but she was one. Her husband, Starr's stepfather, had died earlier and now she lived alone in her large house without the financial ability to maintain it or pay the taxes as they came due.

It seemed beneficial for her mother to sell her house and move in with her daughter and grandchildren at Big Sir. This would provide Starr the needed financing to build the deli and would help her greatly with having a family member tending to the children during the day.

Grandma Light was also a musician, she sang and played the piano, wrote verses and painted portraits. After her passing, one of her self-portraits hung in the waiting area at the Big Sur Deli.

The Rabbit in the Moon

In Chinese literature, rabbits accompany Chang'e, the Chinese goddess of the moon

San Luis Obispo is a college town with oodles of head shops, bars, health food stores and sushi bars, not to mention the street vendors and musicians, the sort of thing that Steve was familiar with not too long ago coming from Indiana State. He immediately felt at home, parked his F120 on Higuera Street and began to check it all out.

It was mid-afternoon, and all that he had eaten this day were the two cheese Danish back at Big Sur, so he soon found himself positioned on a bar stool at the counter of Taco Grande taking on a large shrimp wrap, which by his estimation must have weighed at least a couple pounds.

With his lunch complete, he headed on down the street, arriving at a bizarre attraction called Bubble Gum Alley. In the early 1960s, a few wads of gum had appeared stuck on a wall in the alley, then more and more. By the 1970s, the shop owners complained and demanded the gum be cleaned off, but it was too late because the gum just kept appearing.

Before returning to the truck, he came across a phone booth, and he remembered that he had promised to call Moon.

"Hello, Moon, it's me, Steve, Steven Benet, the guy with the rabbit."

"Oh, hi! Steve, how did it go? Did you see Jordan?

"Yes, and he fixed Trudy up just as you said—about an hour ago. I got a bite to eat, and I ended up checking out this Bubble Gum Alley. It's the weirdest thing, gum all over the walls."

"Yes, I've seen it before. Say, Steve, I was wondering, about the rabbit, Trudy. I could take care of her for you. Why don't you bring her back to Big Sur? There's some wood and chicken wire in the shed, and you could make a pen. I'll nurse her back to health, and when you're ready to return from your trip to the south, you could pick her up."

"Are you sure? I don't want to be an inconvenience for you."

It was approaching dinnertime when Steve returned from San Luis. He was beginning to feel awkward with the situation that was unfolding. He had no particular interest in the rabbit other than his feeling bad about having run over it and his hopes that it would get better. Certainly, if he weren't finding Moon so attractive, he would probably not have agreed to build the pen and would have simply moved on.

When he arrived, Moon was standing outside waiting, ready to receive him and Trudy.

The Big Sur Deli and its attendant residence were situated next to the Post Office. The residence was located off to the side behind the deli and hidden by several redwood trees. It was a two-story wood-framed building covered with gray cedar board and bat siding with all the bedrooms on the upper floor.

At her insistence, they walked to the house, entered through the back door, climbed the three steps to the main floor, walked back the long hallway to the front of the house and entered the living room to the left. Starr was sitting near the front bay window gazing intently into her crystal ball.

Moon whispered to Steve, "Wait for her to acknowledge us. It will only take a moment."

Starr turned slowly toward them, and then began to rise. "Hello, Moon. I haven't seen you all day. And who do we have here?"

Steve was more than surprised. He stood watching her with his hands in his rear pockets. Her mother was beautiful: tall, with long sandy hair hanging down her front and back, wearing a star-speckled bohemian maxi dress with an empire waist and full angel sleeves gathered into cuffs.

"Mother, I would like for you to meet Steve Franks. He has come to us with an injured rabbit. Steve, this is Starr, my mother."

"Hello, Steve. I am pleased to meet you. An injured rabbit, she says. How did you come across it?"

"I'm sorry to say that I hit it with my truck. It was foggy and I didn't see it." He wobbled slightly as he spoke.

"And you rescued it, didn't you? Not everyone would stop for an injured lagomorph."

Moon explained to her mother how Steve had taken the rabbit to Jordan at Cal Poly that morning and of their plan for him to leave the rabbit with her until he returned from Cathedral City, and that he would build a pen for the rabbit in the morning.

Following dinner, Moon and Steve finished the dishes, put everything away and walked out to the beach below. It was high tide and there was practically no beach at all, so they sat on the rocks and poked around looking for creatures in the pockets of water trapped in the crevices while at the same time dodging the waves that continuously crashed against the jagged crags.

Later that evening, Steve took his sleeping bag from the back of his pickup, found a dry spot near the top of the rocks and spread it out on the sandy beach. Moon returned to the house and prepared herself for bed. Trudy remained on the passenger seat of the truck, and Starr gazed intently at her crystal ball.

Steve undressed down to his underwear, climbed inside his sleeping bag and listened to the surf crash on the rocks below. He thought about how each day the earth battled the moon for the ocean, a gravitational tug-of-war with the ocean's water that the earth always won. He was close enough that he could feel the ocean spray, and with his outstretched arm, he grabbed a handful of sand before falling asleep.

The following morning he awoke to the sound of the shrieking gulls and terns and saw that the tide had receded. The gray blanket of fog that covered the landscape was cheating him, he thought, of its break of day warmth. He quickly scrambled to get dressed and hauled his bag of groceries and charcoal from the back of his truck to his campsite. After hurriedly squeezing a stream of Coleman lighter fluid onto the mound of charcoal, he struck a match and watched the yellow-blue flame reverberate above the sand. Once the red glow of the coals became well distributed, he flattened the mound clearing a circular bare spot in the center where he placed an opened can of pinto beans and sank it slightly into the sand to keep it from spilling. With his pocketknife, he whittled a point on a green sapling, inserted it into the end of one of his frankfurters and held it over the coals, rotating it slowly until the wiener became puffed and slightly charred. He then withdrew it from the spit and neatly tucked it into a waiting hot-dog bun. As he sat spooning out the heated pinto beans from the can while balancing the frankfurter sandwich on his lap, Moon climbed down to his campsite bringing with her a pot of coffee and two cups.

Following breakfast, Steve was anxious to get started, and Moon led him out to the shed where the materials for the rabbit cage were stored. He had sketched a schematic in his mind about how he was going to assemble it, subject of course to the materials and what supplies were on hand.

There were plenty of staples and chicken wire. The problem was that the only lumber was 2 x 4 inch boards. He had hoped for something lighter like 2 X 2s. He found a rusty handsaw and a claw hammer and went to work, and after two hours, it was finished.

He placed the newly built cage on the veranda and retrieved Trudy from the front seat of his truck, where she waited patiently for her new quarters to be completed. Moon brought out some containers for water and vegetables and placed them into the cage. Once inside, Trudy seated herself on a pile of straw as the three of them stared back and forth at each other.

Steve carried the remains of his groceries back to the truck. He returned to the veranda thinking that this would be the last time that he would see Trudy, and then he walked to the main house to say goodbye to Starr, and to thank her for her hospitality.

She answered his rap at the back door and invited him in. Their eyes met and he unconsciously looked down returning slowly to meet her gaze. She watched closely as he spoke, noticing each of his mannerisms, how he shuffled his feet and put his hands in his hip pockets, thinking that he seemed unpolished, having been an Army officer.

"Steve, I couldn't help but notice you last night. You seem bright, honest and hardworking as well as full of compassion, at least for a certain rabbit that you're leaving behind. Then this morning I just finished admiring the cage you built, and I realized that you're quite talented. I must admit that I questioned your judgment when I learned that you had enrolled into the ROTC program and had gone to Iraq; but who am I to judge? Little do I know. I probably have no business telling you this and you can probably figure it out for yourself, but my daughter Moon has a certain fondness for you.

"The winter rains have started early this year. Moreover, we have a serious roof problem here. I know that you would like to continue on to Cathedral City to see your dad that you haven't seen for a long time. Nevertheless, Sirius is off to Monterey today ordering a truckload of heavy shakes for a new roof, and I would expect that we would receive delivery possibly sometime next week. Is there any chance that I can talk you into remaining here for a while and helping out with the roof? I can give you room and board while you're here working, but other than that I can't promise you anything."

He wobbled for a moment and realized that he did want very much to stay. Looking downward he spoke, "Yes. I'd be very happy to help you."

The roof materials wouldn't arrive until the end of next week, Moon and Sirius were both occupied all day tending to the Big Sur Deli, and Starr, well she was always occupied with her many activities. Steve was feeling tired and irritable from having nothing to do.

He picked up a copy of the Monterey Herald and scanned each page looking for anything that might catch his attention. Then, in a square box, it seemed to jump out at him. He folded it open, then in half, then in half again. He read the ad aloud.

"MONTEREY => SANTA BARBARA. Californian skipper, mid-60s, looking for crew to help me sail my solid well-equipped 42' sailboat from Monterey to Santa Barbara, Calif. Leaving mid-October. You must be easygoing and flexible with a good sense of humor. Previous offshore experience and other boating skills (e.g. cooking, mechanical) would be an asset. For more info, email me at cptbob@yahoo.com or call at 381-443-2230, ask for Captain Bob."

Steve had never been on a sailboat let alone served as a member of a crew. The ad didn't say that boating skills were required, only that they would be an asset. *You never know,* he thought to himself, *but I have nearly a week.* He was a little apprehensive, but it all sounded good.

Moon stepped out on the veranda just to see how he was doing and took a seat. He handed her the paper. "Take a look at this. You never know, it might be a good opportunity."

She hated to see him leave, even for only a week, but she also knew that there was nothing happening for him there. "It sounds like quite an adventure. I suppose you ought to check it out. When you return, you'll have to take the Amtrak train to Salinas. From there you can take the Salinas-Monterey Transit to Big Sur."

Sirius was in need of help, and Moon returned inside. Steve found a pay phone in the office and spent nearly an hour attempting to contact Captain Bob in Monterey at the number in the ad. When he finally got through, he was told that he was out on the boat. He asked about the ad for a crewmember, and the woman on the phone said that it was still open. He left a message that he was coming the next day to meet Captain Bob.

That night he was too excited to sleep, and he walked over to the kitchen at the deli hoping to get a glass of milk. As he walked past the kitchen, the phone rang, but he was too late and the phone stopped ringing. Then the whir of the fax machine began, and out came a letter from Captain Bob spelling out the precise time and place to meet him.

Steve ambled out the back door of the kitchen, onto the veranda and then down the path that led to the rocky cliff. There he took a seat on a large boulder brightly illuminated by the overhead moon. As the tide slowly worked its way out, he was thinking how he was slowly working his way down the coast. If he hadn't agreed to help with the roof, he would have been able to continue on to Cathedral City from Santa Barbara. He hated to admit it, but it said something about his priorities.

He woke up the next morning with Moon standing at the open door to his room dressed in Levis and an orange, long-sleeved, satin blouse with frill detail on the neck and cuffs and a bright smile. "I'm ready; let's go," speaking good-humoredly and as if she knew his plans.

Steve did a double take. "How do you know?"

"I dreamed it last night."

"About the trip to Santa Barbara?"

"Yes." She spoke teasingly, "I saw you on this two-masted sailboat. A storm came up and you took charge of the wheel; it was over quickly and everything was all right; otherwise, I wouldn't want you to go." She paused and then said, speaking slightly puzzled, "There was something else; I saw us standing in the middle of an artichoke field, It was late in the afternoon, and the fog was covering everything; we were there with several farm workers, sharing a meal with them. That's all that I remember."

With the Pacific Ocean on their left, the aged Ford pickup sped along Highway 1, Steve behind the wheel and Moon in the passenger seat.

Sirius had returned from Monterey reporting that the roofing materials wouldn't arrive for two more weeks, not one as expected. Moon hadn't had a day off from the Deli for over a month, and she was enjoying the ride except for the uncertainty that she felt about his leaving. Starr had covered for Sirius while he was in Monterey, and today he had to cover for Moon. Apart from having seen them together in the artichoke field, there was no certainty that he would return.

The winding highway wound its way around the twisting coastline, and they soon arrived at the spot where Steve had nearly missed running into the landslide days earlier. He noticed that all the debris had been removed. He was no expert, but it appeared to him that the hillside remained dubiously subject to further erosion with the coming rains. All along the way, water seeped down from the hillside onto the highway leaving zebra stripes on the bleached gray asphalt.

After a half-hour or so, they pulled into the Monterey Marina. It was a large parking lot and Captain Bob's faxed instructions told them precisely where to park in order to easily locate the boat.

Steve turned the ignition to its off position while the engine continued to turn over a few more times, causing the truck to shake. "That's why folks use the term, 'kill the engine,'" implying that there was some force under the hood fiercely strangling the powerful motor, some hoary ogre with padded palms grabbing the hot power plant with both hands and arms and hanging on. He had a similar vision that whenever he applied pressure on the brake pedal that that same ogre lowered his feet to the pavement bringing the vehicle to a halt. When the truck sat idle, that is when the ogre slept. He would sleep with his feet resting on two bicycle pedals waiting for someone to turn the ignition. Turning the key sent a spark to the ogre telling him to wake up and to start peddling which turned over the engine. Voila!

Moon was unimpressed with his story. Her thoughts centered on his leaving and her fear that he wouldn't return. *How could he be joking?* she wondered, while feeling sorry for herself. She remembered when Jordan had left for Cal Poly; he said that he would return too.

She reached into her knitted handbag and pulled out a small medallion. Then, turning towards Steve, she placed it into his hand and said, "Here, take this. You could use it as kind of a good luck piece—for the storm." She smiled. Mystified, he took the token and looked at it closely. It bore the image of a rabbit within a moon. "It's the rabbit in the moon," she said, "a symbol of friendship."

They both climbed out of the truck and walked over to the railing overlooking the pier where Captain Bob's cruiser Bobby Magill remained berthed. He soon spotted the boat and saw two men on the deck, one fussing with the rigging and the other washing the portholes. Steve handed her the keys to the pickup, thanked her for coming along with him and for taking the truck back to Big Sur, then he started toward the boat.

"Just a sec," he said turning slowly around. Placing his hands on her shoulders, he kissed her on the forehead. Then he realized that the past four days that he had spent with her had just ended with only a first-date peck on the cheek. He began to experience a feeling in his chest that he hadn't felt for a long time. Sliding his hands downward to her waist and pulling her close, he fervently pressed his lips against hers as she eagerly returned his advance with equal enthusiasm.

The Bobbie Magill

It was a warm, sunny day at the Monterey Marina and Steve could hear the shriek of the gulls and terns as well as the barking seals and sea lions under the pier at Fisherman's Wharf. In the distance beyond the boat-filled harbor, he could see the opposite side of the bay where Fort Ord was hidden beyond the beach and tree line. In the harbor, there were various types of vessels including small dinghies, fishing boats of an assortment of shapes and sizes with nets and rigging; and there were more than a few yachts parked farther out.

He walked down the pier casually examining each craft until he arrived at the Bobby Magill, where Captain Bob and one other fellow were both busy at work. He called out to the man wearing the captain's hat. "Captain Bob?"

"Yes, that would be me," stopping what he was doing.

Captain Bob was tall, and appeared to be in his early sixties. Patches of gray were overrunning the wavy blond hair sticking out from beneath his hat; he appeared to be slightly overweight. "Ahoy, you must be Franks?"

"Yes, Steven Benet Franks. May I come aboard?"

"Yes, yes, we've been wondering if you were going to show. Come on and let's talk." Then, turning and pointing to the other fellow he said, "This guy over here with the paint brush in his hand is Addis Abba. He's going with us as far as San Luis."

Addis Abba stepped down from the stool he was standing on and sat his brush on the side of the can of white paint. Offering his hand to Steve, he spoke with a British accent. "Good to meet you."

"Addis Abba here is from Zimbabwe and he's been accepted at Cal Poly, which is on our way south. He's had some sailing experience on the Great Zambezi and also on the Nile. How about you, Franks, you had any seafaring experience?" questioned Captain Bob.

"No. I was under the impression that you were looking for someone easygoing and flexible with a good sense of humor. I'm certainly all of that. My only experience is a one-year hitch in Iraq. I was just discharged from Fort Ord. I've always wanted to see what sailing was all about, so I certainly have an interest in learning the difference between a half-hitch and a bowline."

"Hmm, infantry, Iraq, Al-Qaeda," speaking to himself. I guess you do have a certain type of experience, even if it is limited to C-rations cooked over Sterno. I would certainly have liked you to have at least some sailing experience, especially since young Addis Abba is getting off at San Luis, but you'll have to do. We'll be leaving first thing in the morning. Bring your gear on and I'll show you where you can stow it."

Steve rightfully assumed that he had passed muster. He carried on board a small duffle bag containing a change of clothes, toiletries, a few other miscellaneous items and a .38 caliber pistol in its leather holster. Before heading down the steps, he looked back and saw Moon standing at the railing by the truck, she returned his wave and blew him a kiss.

Moon waited around hoping to watch the Bobby Magill and its crew sail off into the proverbial sunset. However, when she saw the three of them leave the boat joking together, she realized that they were forming a new friendship, bonding. They were at the beginning of a new adventure. As she watched them walk toward Fisherman's Wharf, most likely for dinner, she felt alone and wished that she were a part of it.

The drive back to Big Sur seemed to her to take forever. As she drove through town, the traffic irritated her. Unsure of how to get to Highway 1 she ended up missing the highway ramp and made her way down Munras Avenue, catching each of the red lights, finally coming to a second access. Pulling on to Highway 1, she remembered again that she was alone. The moon, the ocean and the surrounding cypress all conspired unsuccessfully to numb her chagrin. How she could have let her defenses down? She wondered. How dare he come into her life as he had and then leave?

Meanwhile, Captain Bob, Addis Abba and Steven Benet all filed into the 'Captain's Gig' at the edge of the wharf and took an outside table. The tables were small so they pulled two of them together. Before ordering food, they went through two pitchers of Sierra Nevada Ale and four baskets of sour dough bread.

Occasionally they had to fight off the gulls that would dive bomb from time to time whenever they saw an opening like when one of them once went off to the head to take a piss or when the three of them started tossing bread off the edge down to a barking seal below.

After ordering the third pitcher, they decided on three large Captain's platters with deep-fried shrimp, calamari, oysters, and scallops and a double order of garlic fries for each of them. Then for desert, there was a fourth and then a fifth pitcher.

When the proprietor notified them that his staff had left a half-hour earlier, that the wharf was empty except for a few hangers-on and that he was closing, they were blasted drunk. Captain Bob responded to the owner's plea by offering up a $50 bill, but to no avail.

After two more attempts, the owner called the local security. In a matter of minutes, four security guards, of which three were males and one was female, arrived on the scene each wearing side arms with billy clubs in hand.

All that the three would have had to do to have gotten out of this confrontation was to quietly leave and return to the boat. Nevertheless, Captain Bob made a remark about the female officer, "…with the tight ass and perky tits." The three were quickly seized, frisked, handcuffed, loaded into a waiting paddy wagon and sent downtown to the drunk tank.

Inside the wagon, the three of them laughed and joked most of the way to the station agreeing that this was a great way to start a great adventure, a sign of good things to come. After all, they barely knew each other; they had just met; and look how much fun they were having! Steve then noticed there were others in the wagon: two prostitutes.

"Hey! Check this out. We've got company," Steve announced.

The two girls both sat stone-faced trying to ignore the guys and any forthcoming remarks. However, that didn't dissuade Captain Bob, who seemed to be the nucleus of this evening's adventure. Laughing while talking, he looked at the tall blonde-haired person and said, "Hey honey, why don't you come over and sit next to me?"

She snapped back coldly, "Mister, why don't you mind your own business?"

The brown-haired woman, who was a little shorter, chimed in, "Yeah, can't you see we're headed for jail? Just take it easy."

Captain Bob then said to Steve, "I can work with the brunette, why don't you take the blond. She's a real tiger."

About that time, the window separating the driver and his guard in the front seat slid open. The guard shouted back, "You guys take it easy or you're heading into real trouble."

Captain Bob slurred back, "What you gonna do, put us in jail? I thought that's where we're headed anyhow."

Addis Abba and Steve were both starting to sober a little and were beginning to realize that the Captain wasn't helping their cause any. They wouldn't have been in this wagon except for his mouth. The two looked at each other and silently agreed that they were never going to get out of this unless they could get the Captain to be quiet.

The wagon stopped at the rear of the police station, and the three guys were led in, booked, fingerprinted and sent to the tank. They were each relieved of the contents of their pockets as well as their belts and shoestrings.

The holding cell was large and contained several others of the same intoxicated persuasion. (The Monterey Jail wasn't yet co-ed.) There was one seat remaining, and Steve offered it to Addis Abba, who accepted it while Captain Bob and Steve both took to the floor and soon fell asleep.

The next morning they were sent to the Municipal Court, where they agreed to pay the fine and costs for disorderly conduct and were released after they made payment using their credit cards.

As they walked out the front door, the two women from the previous night were waiting for them in front of the courthouse. Captain Bob, appearing a little embarrassed, was quick to make amends and offered his most sincere apology.

"What happened last night, well, we were celebrating. We were preparing for our sendoff. We're sailing from here today—down the coast to Santa Barbara—and I guess, no not guess, I had too much to drink, and the cops were right in hauling me in. Could I buy you a cup of coffee, breakfast or something?"

"It seems all right to me. I could use a cup of coffee and croissant; how about you, Havana?"

Havana smiled and said, "OK, Lacey, it sounds good to me. Where do you guys want to go?"

Captain Bob suggested, "Let's just walk down Alvarado Street, towards the wharf. I'm sure we can find a place. By the way," (while tipping his hat) "I'm Captain Bob, and these two guys: that's Steve Benet Franks and this is Addis Abba."

Lacey was the tall blond and of the two she was the one that had seemed most unfriendly last night, but today she led the conversation. "I'm Lacey Cupertino, and this is my friend Havana Charpantier." They all shook hands with each other and soon arrived at the front door of the Broken Egg Café.

Breakfast was more than a cup of coffee and a croissant. After huevos rancheros and Portuguese linguini, café lattes and mimosas, the group had loosened up and Lacey and Havana decided to sign on as additional crew of the Bobby Magill. They only needed an hour or so to round up some clothes and essentials for the trip.

The three guys walked onto the boat astonished at this turn of events, wondering if the girls really were going to show. By noon, Lacey and Havana arrived looking like two college girls leaving for spring break in Tijuana.

The sloop was a Hallberg-Rassy 42, manufactured in Ellös Sweden. Captain Bob was an auto dealer who lived in Santa Barbara and had been looking, for some time, for a used sailboat. A broker from Monterey knew of his quest and notified him when this boat became available. It was love at first sight for Bob, and he immediately took possession.

It was now 10:00 in the morning the following day. Captain Bob preferred not to sail at night, and the first leg of the trip was to take them to San Simeon, some eighty to ninety nautical kilometers, which he estimated to take about fourteen hours. Nevertheless, everyone was anxious to get going, and by noon, the Bobby Magill taxied out of the harbor into the bay.

With Addis Abba cleaning up the dock lines and putting up the mainsail and Bob at the helm, they proceeded past Cannery Row, Lover's Point, then the lighthouse at Point Pinos, Assilomar and Pebble Beach. It was a beautiful day with tranquil seas and ten to fifteen knots of wind coming from both the northwest and the southwest. After reaching Point Sur, the course changed to a more southeast direction, and Steve looked through binoculars hoping to get a glimpse of the Big Sur Deli.

You could almost hear the sizzle as the evening sun slowly slipped into the ocean, leaving behind a bright orange sky filled with blue and gray low-level clouds. Captain Bob left Addis Abba at the helm, went below and began making bologna sandwiches and heating up a pot of clam chowder.

He turned on the weather channel on the VHF covering Northern California and then switched it to the Southern California channel, which started to come in. The report indicated that a storm was beginning to form and would probably cross paths with the Bobby Magill later on, most likely after midnight. They would probably be positioned around Lopez Point, near Lucia at that hour.

After serving Steve, Havana and Lacey his freshly heated chowder in the galley, Bob carried two bowls up on the deck, one for himself and one for Addis Abba. Bob continued to hang around the helm with Addis Abba as they both ate their chowder while using autopilot. Steve remained below and visited with Lacey while Havana took a nap.

He told her about him being released from the army and the beginning of his trip to see his father in Cathedral City, how it had been interrupted by his running over the rabbit and his meeting Moon at Big Sur. Lacey enjoyed listening to Steve's tale and began to share her own story.

Her father had been in the diplomatic corps, assigned to various stations around the world. Shuffled from place to place, school to school her parents had put her into a private boarding school in Connecticut and sent funds regularly to the administrators there to cover her tuition and expenses.

One night, on a flight from Zurich to Madrid, the small aircraft that they were passengers on went down, killing them both.

She then went to live with her uncle in Cleveland, who had been appointed by the court as her legal guardian until the age of twenty-one. The proceeds of her parent's life insurance policy were placed into a trust fund with her uncle being named as the trustee. By the time Lacey reached the age of twenty-one, her uncle had totally depleted the trust fund, and Lacey was broke. The winters in Connecticut and Ohio were cold, and she had decided to try her luck in California.

The first evidence that the weather was beginning to change was when a dark fog began to close in. Then the wind began increasing and the swells began to pick up, causing the boat to rock from side to side. Storm clouds began filling the sky, white caps dotted the ocean, the deep-sea began churning and stirring and the waters became rough.

Captain Bob gave instructions to everyone not to go below deck or to the head. If there were to be any vomiting it was to be done off the stern. As the fog thickened, the visibility dropped to less than a quarter of a mile and Bob navigated the way using radar, autopilot and a horn blasting every two minutes. The storm was both terrifying and exhilarating. He seemed to be taking it all in his stride and then he did something nobody expected, he asked Steve to take over the helm.

"Just keep your eyes on the compass," he shouted and then took a seat next to Addis Abba.

"Are you sure you don't want to take her?" he repeated several times. Captain Bob continued checking his chart and their GPS coordinates always mindful of their safety. He was concerned about not drifting too close to the shoreline where the rocky crags posed a serious danger.

"No, you're doing just fine. It isn't as bad as it seems; it's just a squall, a short-lived commotion. It'll blow over in a short time, maybe a half hour or so."

Steve reached in his pocket for the medallion Moon had given him and clutched it tightly while keeping his eyes on the compass. For a moment he thought that he could hear her speaking to him, telling him that the storm would soon be over and that all would be safe. The twelve-foot seas rocked and rolled longer than Bob had expected, and Steve continued checking his watch hoping that the gale would soon let up.

In spite of Captain Bob's instructions about remaining on deck, Havana remained below trying her best to sleep, which consisted mostly of keeping her eyes closed while waiting for the next swell to toss her from one side of the bed to the other. Her stomach was turning, and at times, she felt as though she might vomit.

As she drifted in and out of sleep, it was difficult for her to distinguish when she was awake or dreaming. The squall reminded her of another time, when she was in a small boat, in the middle of a storm with the rain beating down and the wind blowing.

She had managed to row her small dory to the pier of her uncle's house. It was in the Bayou and she had to steer around the large mangrove roots that interwove together like the threads in a tapestry. The storm continued to rage and pour buckets of rain onto her tired, thin malnourished body. She climbed from the small boat onto the pier and banged on the wooden door hoping to be let in. Above the sound of the rain pelting against the porch roof she could barely hear Tante answering, "*Entrez!*"

As soon as she slid the lever, the door swung inward easily with the help of the wind, and she quickly dashed inside feeling the warmth held therein coming from the fire in the stone fireplace on the opposite wall. Tante was sitting in a rocking chair next to the flames with her large dog asleep at her feet. Oncle and her cousin sat at the table a few feet away. All three had been drinking heavily and there was a half-filled whiskey bottle on the table with several empties lying about. An iron kettle of gumbo pretended to keep warm sitting next to the fire.

Havana helped herself to the overcooked sticky gumbo using the spoon on a hook next to the kettle. She hadn't eaten for a day and a half. She took a seat at the table and began to eat, holding the bowl with her hands and spooning the thick food into her mouth with her fingers. Oncle offered to pour her some whiskey, and she accepted. They all continued to drink. Soon the bottle was empty, and Oncle replaced it with a full one.

The rain, lightening and thunder continued along with the night. Tante could see that Havana was now drunk and she broke the silence looking at her husband and son, "Well, which one of you wants to do her?"

Oncle looked at his fourteen-year-old son and offered, "This must be your first, *mon fils*; you take her and then I'll follow." His gaze turned toward Havana and he looked directly into her eyes thinking that he would get a positive response. Seeing only a blank stare, he climbed from his stool and stumbled toward her, grabbing her by the throat.

Havana was sober enough to know what was happening to her and complained a little, but she was weak and didn't offer much resistance. The two forced her onto the floor in front of the fireplace, and then her cousin pulled her legs apart and raised her skirt. In a quick moment, it was over, and his father laughed. He then put the whiskey bottle to her lips and forced it down her throat until she began to vomit. The gumbo spewed forth onto her clothing and the floor and the dog began to clean it up.

Oncle continued to laugh and asked, "Mama, do you think the dog would want to do her?" Her uncle and cousin held the dog in position, but it refused, and when it got the chance, it scampered away.

Havana finally passed out after her uncle abused her, raping and clawing her for close to an hour. The two took their turns with her several more times until neither of them could continue.

The next morning she discovered that her dress was so mutilated that Tante gave her a shirt and a pair of pants. Havana left the Bayou never to return.

Eventually, Steve felt the seas subside a bit, and he was able to relax his grip and catch his breath. After the storm ended, Captain Bob realized that they had drifted quite far from the coastline and changed course heading back towards land. The GPS equipment had malfunctioned. He confessed that they had been thrown off course. Relying on his compass, he headed the boat toward land. Eventually they arrived at San Simeon, pulled into the harbor and tied up for the balance of the night.

The next morning they awoke and saw the beach and the small town consisting mainly of a church and a restaurant that posed additionally as a general store. Perched on a mountain in the distance they could see Hearst Castle.

Havana was ready to quit. She had had enough sailing and announced that she was going to catch a bus and return to Monterey.

Captain Bob located a specialist in San Simeon to work on the GPS. The problem was very minor, a loose cable, and after a quick breakfast, the remaining four headed out toward Morro Bay, the shortest leg of their trip. There was to be no storm, but the waters were to remain somewhat rough.

Once they were on their way, Steve and Addis Abba both sat together while Steve began the conversation. "So, you are getting off at Morro Bay?"

"Yes. As you know, I am from Zimbabwe. I have been accepted into the university there at San Luis Obispo, The College of Agriculture at California Polytechnic State University.

"I've heard of Zimbabwe, but I can't say that I know exactly where it is."

"Southern Africa, between South Africa and Zambia; you may possibly know my country as Rhodesia."

"So, you're a long way from home. Is this your first time in America?"

"Actually I was here several months ago, when I arrived in order to determine for myself if this would be a good place for me to go to school. I do like it here very much. The weather is much cooler than in my home, however, it is very enjoyable. I was wondering; have you ever been to Africa?"

"No, I haven't. Actually, I haven't been very many places in the world, only Iraq. I just returned from there, the military."

"Yes, I understand. I guess I am not very comfortable discussing politics, not being from here, you see. Nevertheless, I am curious, and excuse me if I am out of line, but what are your feelings about the war?"

"I have always supported the president, and even though I don't like the war, I believe it's my duty to answer the call of my country. Tell me, it seems as if many African countries are struggling. Is that so for Zimbabwe?"

"Zimbabwe is living on a time bomb. Observers predict an implosion if our present dictator continues with his hard-line policies that have destroyed the economy. Agriculture, once a mainstay of Zimbabwe's economy, has dramatically declined because of chaotic farm invasions, drought, lack of inputs and skilled labor. This has also led to the critical shortages of foreign currency and low, if non-existent investment.

"Drought, floods and economic problems have reduced Zimbabwe's agricultural output this year while a controversial, often violent land reform program, has made it difficult for thousands of people to access food. It is my hope that I can learn something from you Americans at one of your fine universities about agriculture. I want to know how to grow food, how to finance the production of food, how to market and distribute it. Perhaps, if I, along with others from my country, can bring back some of your knowledge, we will be better equipped to get our country back on its feet again.

"UN sanctions and a guerrilla uprising finally led to free elections in 1979 and independence (as Zimbabwe) in 1980. Robert Mugabe, our nation's first prime minister, has been the country's only ruler (as president since 1987) and has dominated the country's political system since independence. His chaotic land redistribution campaign begun in 2000, caused an exodus of white farmers, crippled the economy, and ushered in widespread shortages of basic commodities. Ignoring international condemnation, Mugabe rigged the 2002 presidential election to ensure his reelection. I must tell you, opposition and labor groups launched general strikes in 2003 in an attempt to pressure Mugabe to retire early, but they were quickly put down by security forces."

It didn't take long for them to arrive at their next stop, Morro Bay, a working fishing village. Juan Rodriguez Cabrillo named its famous landmark, Morro Rock, when he first charted this coast during his 16th Century voyage of discovery. The town is a pleasant tourist destination, which has very mild weather all year long. There is no such thing as traffic in Morro Bay, unless of course, you count birds, sea mammals, and fish!

Upon arrival, Addis Abba disembarked for Cal Poly while Steve, Captain Bob and Lacey parked the boat to go ashore for lunch. After lunch, they walked around town. Steve noticed that Captain Bob and Lacey were holding hands as they walked. Steve hoped that he could show them the Bubble Gum Alley in nearby San Luis Obispo, however, they went to the beach and spent the afternoon sunbathing and swimming instead.

Hoping to get an early start the next morning, they returned to the boat, and Captain Bob checked his charts and the weather report. All indications were that the inclement weather had passed, and they could expect calm and tranquil seas the following day, all the way to Santa Barbara.

They had reached the halfway point to their destination. They would be sailing the remaining part of their journey beginning the following day and continuing through the next night until the following mid-morning when they should arrive in Santa Barbara.

Bob and Lacey went below taking the cabin in the aft. Steve went to his cabin near the bow, undressed and climbed in between the clean white sheets. He wasn't used to going to bed that early and wasn't tired. He remained restless, unable to fall asleep. His thoughts centered first on the crazy night of sailing during the storm between Big Sur and San Simeon, how Captain Bob had trusted him to take the helm during the frightening squall.

He thought about all that Addis Abba had related to him about Zimbabwe and the struggle of that nation. Steve was envious of Addis Abba. He had direction, a meaningful purpose in life. He knew what he wanted to accomplish and he had a plan to bring it about. He had somehow managed to break away and not be a part of the problem, but part of the solution.

He then thought about Captain Bob and Lacey in the other cabin, what they must be doing right now. Lacey was several years older than Steve and quite a lot younger than Captain Bob. She looked great though. He had seen her in her bikini at the beach that afternoon. Bob and Lacey were getting along quite well together. They swam, laughed and played together as if they had known each other for a long time. He conjectured that if Havana hadn't gotten off the boat at San Simeon, she might be sharing the bed with him that night.

He thought about Moon, reached for his trousers on the floor next to his bed and retrieved the medallion that she had given him, a symbol of friendship. He then remembered how she had kissed him after dropping him off back at the marina in Monterey. When she had reached for him and he put his arms around her, he could feel the shape of her back, her waist, her hair draping both her front and back; he could taste her lips and smell her sweet fragrance.

She was certainly reason enough to return to Big Sur. But what then? He would return, help with the new roof and then be on his way. There would be no reason for him stay after the roof was on. He couldn't stay. Big Sur was too small. There were no jobs for him there. How could he earn a living?

He looked out the window of his cabin, and he could see the moon shining brightly. Staring intently, he could almost make out what generations of people throughout the world had seen before him, the rabbit in the moon. It was somewhat of a twisted configuration with the main part of its body on the left side, the head at the top and the long ears curving around to the right end of the orb.

As he lay on the soft bed, he could feel the gentle swaying of the Bobbie Magill. The yacht drifted slightly about its mooring, and the moon wafted from his view. In a matter of moments, Steve floated into a deep slumber that would carry him until the next morning.

He awoke feeling the movement of the boat rising and then lowering in synchronization with the motion of the ocean swells. His blanket and top sheet were on the floor evidencing a tumultuous night. The sound of the Bobby Magill's auxiliary engine, a turbo-charged 76 HP Volvo marine diesel, which drove an 18" 3-bladed Max-Prop, could be heard signaling to him that they were on their way. Looking out the window from his bunk, he could see that he had slept through dawn. Bright sunshine blasted its way through the porthole and onto his face.

Suddenly he heard the auxiliary engine go silent followed by the snap of the sails being unfurled and catching the northwest breeze. He felt the boat lean to its side in response to the wind pressing the threesome southward toward the coastal town of Santa Barbara.

As he reached for his trousers, he realized he was still clutching his medallion and slipped it into his pants pocket. He quickly dressed and passed through the galley on his way to the steps up to the deck, grabbing a banana on the way.

Pulling himself upward by the handrails, his head and face penetrated the outside air; feeling the shock of the cool, gentle ocean wind. As he looked around, the clear sky reflected the blue waters below dotted with occasional spots of white caps. Lacey was at the helm. Captain Bob was adjusting the sails, and two gulls hovered over the sloop as it carved its way through the highway to anywhere. From the direction of the stern, he could see the giant Morro Rock fading away. To the port side he watched as bathers were arriving at Pismo Beach, couples, and parents with children carrying sand buckets and shovels. He could see the lifeguards taking their stations on the wooden platforms and the beach crews carrying out kayaks and placing them near the water's edge.

Once out of the bay, with Captain Bob's help, Lacey turned the boat south toward Point Argüelles. Bob took a seat next to Steve and started the conversation. "So, tell me about Iraq. You are the first person I've come across that's served there."

"I was assigned to the 102 Armored Division. It was our job to secure the area known as Kirkuk. After I'd been there eight months, I was in a jeep going from Kirkuk to Bagdad when we were attacked. Just as the jeep I was riding in hit a road mine, you know, an IED, an improvised exploding devise, we began receiving machine gun fire coming from a building top. The explosion threw me into the air and I landed behind an armored personnel carrier. It hurled me so forcefully that I ended up with two broken ribs and a broken arm. I guess you can say I was lucky. A lot of others haven't been so fortunate."

Steven continued. "It wasn't just the hostilities that made it so bad. It didn't take long for me to begin tiring of the sand always blowing in my face, the intense heat, the hard cot that I slept on every night. There was the look on their Iraqi faces, which was a look of distrust, the look that revealed that they didn't like me, that they didn't want me to be there. They didn't throw flowers before my path. In fact I was rarely on the path, except when on duty, because it wasn't safe. I was always on the lookout, watching every step for fear of stepping on a mine, which happened anyhow. I missed going to the movies, going out for a beer; and girls, how much I missed the girls. You have no idea how much I wanted to be with a woman. Then there were the repeated reminders by the CO of our successes, reminders that the enemy was gradually being defeated and that we were bringing freedom to a people who hadn't know freedom for the past forty years."

Bob reached into the cooler and withdrew two bottles of Sierra Nevada Ale handing one to Steve and twisting the top off the other. Bob remarked, "This is starting to sound really serious. Perhaps you should try this on for size."

Steve said, "You're right, I guess I was getting carried away. Somehow, things just didn't seem to add up. If we were the captors, why then did I feel as if we were the captured?"

Bob responded, "Being a soldier has never been easy. In Nam, I was with the Riverines in the Mekong Delta. Our job was a joint effort between the Army and Navy. We would ride up and down the snake infested rivers and canals hoping to draw fire from Charley, draw him out in the open. Then we would leave the boats behind and chase after him on foot. We were always wet, covered with leaches and the skin on the soles of our feet would be so rotten that it would come off with our socks. The mosquitoes kept us from sleeping.

"I know what you mean about loneliness and wanting to be with a woman. While I was there, I had my share of whores: young ones, old ones, it made no difference. It wasn't rape; they did if for the money. But the look on their faces: sullen, dull and gray, like the clouds overhead, never a genuine smile or grin. Sometimes I just wanted to talk, to be able to say, you and I, can't we just put this war aside for a few minutes and be friends?"

Bob realized that he too was becoming a little too sentimental. He chugged the balance of his beer, reached for two more, then arched his back and released a grand belch. "Damn! Why does that always feel so damn good?"

While twisting off the cap on his second brusky he continued, "But we, you and I, we're the survivors. We did our duty, and we have nothing to be ashamed of. We have every right to be proud. Here lieutenant, have another beer on me."

Then Captain Bob paused, took a long gulp of beer, looked firmly at Steve and said, "I guess the one thing that never settled well with me was this: 2,000,000 Vietnamese and 50,000 Americans died in a war designed by our President and Congress to prevent the Communist dominoes from falling: Viet Nam, Laos, Cambodia and then Indonesia. When we pulled out, Saigon fell to the NVA and the Viet Cong; still, the dominoes didn't fall. Viet Nam seems to be doing quite well today without us."

The mood began to change, and Steve went below to the galley and prepared himself a peanut butter sandwich, then went to his cabin. He wasn't used to drinking two beers in the morning and certainly not before having anything to eat. He was feeling lightheaded and lay down for a moment. He closed his eyes and then heard a swooshing sound. He felt the wind rush over his body.

He opened his eyes and was surprised to see Lacey sitting in a lotus position on what appeared to be a Persian flying carpet about a foot over the bed. This, of course, made no sense to him, and he passed it off as a dream; but no matter how hard he tried, he was unable to wake up. He yelled out and kicked, but to no avail. Lacey remained smiling, beckoning him to climb aboard, but he resisted, demanding that she leave him alone.

He had seen her on the beach the previous day and she was most alluring, but now she was even more so. Her blond hair was at present coal black and cut in a Cleopatra style pageboy. Her attire was dainty, exposing a jewel in her naval. She appeared as if she had been sent by some Arabian prince from his private harem, meant to lure him to some place that he had always dreamed of but dared not go. Her breasts floated freely about her skimpy top as she leaned forward looking directly into his eyes while motioning for Steve to climb aboard. Her eyes were painted with extreme shades of blue colors outlined in black; she wore bells on her fingers and toes that rang out a cacophony of tingling, vibrating exotic sounds that he had never heard before.

Steve had no control over what he was witnessing. When he surrendered his will, he found himself lying on the soft carpet in the midst of the clouds looking down on the Bobbie Magill, Captain Bob at the helm. Then the boat too disappeared and the only thing visible was Lacey's beauty.

He reached out to touch her, but was unable to, as if she were merely a holographic image projected before him. Nevertheless, when the carpet began to descend from the ether to terra firma, his ears began to pop and he feared that he might fall off the swift moving conveyance.

The carpet landed on an upper level garden terrace overlooking a great city containing a landscape of mosques, minarets, alcazars, courtyards, columns, and domes. He could hear a muezzin issuing a call to prayer from inside a nearby mosque.

Lacey soon disappeared, and Steve found himself surrounded by seven vestal virgins donning white burqahs with gold brocade leading him down a long outdoor gallery, a Moorish type arcade. The virgin to his left loosened her hijab and smiled at him—it was Moon. She then quickly replaced her veil and merged with the other six. Then a second virgin loosened her hijab and winked—it was Havana Charpantier.

When they arrived at the great door, there were two sentries stationed, each standing at attention with AK-47 rifles at their sides. The lead virgin spoke to one of the sentries and then disappeared into space. The remaining virgins, one at a time followed the procedure, each one disappearing like the one before until only Steve remained.

He then found himself in a large auditorium that appeared to be the television set of 'Wheel of Fortune'. Trudy Miller, his girlfriend from Indiana was dressed somewhat like Vanna White and stood near the board ready to light up the letters. Steve stood next to Captain Bob, who was dressed like Pat Sajak, who directed him to spin the wheel. Steve began spinning and guessing the letters as Trudy paced back and forth in front of the board until the words NO MORE WAR were revealed. Then the auditorium lit up with flashing lights, sirens blaring and paratroopers falling from the ceiling.

The archangel Michael appeared with his winged minions, and a great battle ensued. The angels, armed with Arabian scimitars, fought the paratroopers armed with bayonets at the end of their rifles. The audience applauded loudly each time either an angel or a paratrooper fell dead from the sky.

Vanna White and Pat Sajak led Steve out of the set, down a long, dark hallway, down a set of stairs to an elevator that led down several more floors stopping finally at the bottom.

An audible chime sounded as the elevator door opened. Steve looked out into the room and saw a grand round table at which was seated several notable persons. At the head of the table sat Abraham and Moses; to their left sat Jesus Christ, and to their right sat the Prophet Muhammad, each attired in white robes. Then from right to left: Benjamin Franklin, Sadaam Hussein, Woodrow Wilson, Yasser Arafat, Winston Churchill, Ariel Sharon, George Bush, and Osama Bin Laden.

A candelabrum with one lit and twelve unlit candles hung from the ceiling, centered over the table. In the center of the table was a parchment scroll of the Pentateuch, a Holly Bible and Koran.

They all held hands and said a prayer together. "Our Father who art in Heaven, hallowed be thy name."

Then Christ spoke saying, "Peace is not something that can be imposed at the conference table."

Then Muhammad finished the statement, "It can grow only from the hearts of people."

Steve awoke as he felt Lacey shaking him. She said, "Lunch is ready. Why don't you join Bob and me up on deck? We're having cracked crab. Bob picked it up while we were at Morro Bay."

Robert Luis Morrison, also known as Captain Bob, had never been a captain until two weeks ago when he acquired his captain's hat at a souvenir shop on Fisherman's Wharf. Certainly, having registered the title to his $250,000 sailboat with the DMV was all that was needed to justify the commission.

His highest military rank had been staff sergeant E-6. However, at the time of his honorable discharge, he had been busted down to sergeant E-5. This unfortunate reduction was the result of his getting into a scuffle at the NCO club when he popped a corporal in the mouth for making a disparaging remark about his young woman companion.

Bob always seemed to have a difficult time keeping out of trouble. In high school he regularly had to make the trip to the principal's office for disrupting the class, or as was also often the case, fighting. He loved sports, especially playing football, and that was a positive diversion for him. He liked hitting and being hit—he was never afraid to take a punch. Nevertheless, he was very popular in school and was elected homecoming king his senior year. You could ask almost anyone about Bob and they would tell you that he was a good person unless you happened, of course, to be on the wrong side of him that day. Nevertheless, even those guys who had had a run-in with him would soon come around and put past things past and tell you that he was their friend.

In spite of his coarse manner, he was quite playful and commanded the center of attention when among his friends. In addition, he was considered quite handsome having a tall, lean frame, with wavy blond hair. All this, together with an over abundant supply of confidence, made him a real hit with the girls at school, one or two of his feminine teachers, and even a certain mother of one of his friends.

For a while, he had an after-school and Saturday job at Sewell's Market. He stocked shelves, marked prices, sacked groceries and carried bags out to the customers' cars. He liked carrying out groceries the best because he was a good conversationalist, which was good for tips. However, it all ended when Mr. Sewell, the owner, caught him in the stock room late one evening humping one of the checkout girls over a stack of bags of rice.

Bob's father was the owner-operator of Morrison Ford, a small auto dealership in downtown Santa Barbara, and after being fired from Sewell's Market, he went to work at the dealership washing cars, sweeping out the maintenance stalls and other miscellaneous items that would come up during the day.

Bob's pleasing manner with the customers was soon recognized, and his father decided to give him a shot at selling cars from the used-car lot across the street. Bob surprised everyone, including himself. He soon knew that selling was to be his life's work.

Upon graduation from high school, he decided to attend the University of Southern California rather than UC Santa Barbara in order to play football. With his build and speed, he easily made the team as a running back. He also joined the Phi Delta Theta Fraternity and became gold digger's king his senior year. His grades were lousy, but who cared? He could always sell cars, and that was what he did. Returning to his dad's dealership, he became sales manager and eventually took over the business, adding to his growing empire a Toyota dealership.

In between high school, college, Viet Nam, and the car dealership Bob had managed several times to fall in love, get married and then unmarried. He only had one child, to his credit, which was from his first wife, Pamela Jenkins, the checkout girl from Sewell's Market. They named their son James, who turned out to be a near replica of his father, tall, lean with wavy blond hair and a sharp eye for all the good things in life.

James wasn't the punch and kill athlete like his dad and preferred individual sports like surfing and hang gliding off the cliffs of the Santa Ynez Mountains. Nonetheless, he too was a good salesperson and was given reign to the Toyota dealership exactly two weeks before Captain Bob decided on this nautical hiatus that he, Lacey and Steve were enjoying.

"Steve!" Lacey questioned, "When we arrive in Santa Barbara, why not spend a few days together with us? Bob's told me so much about his beautiful home that I can barely wait until we arrive. There's a tennis court, swimming pool, and he has a stable with three horses. I don't understand how he could live all alone, just him and James, in such a large place."

Steve answered, "Perhaps for one day. It sounds great to me, that is, if it isn't too inconvenient. Somehow, I feel like I might be in your way. I've never been to Santa Barbara, and I've always wanted to see the town and the mission there. Father Junipero Serra founded it. I do have to get back to Big Sur; they're waiting on me to help with the roof, you know."

Off, not far, was a small fishing boat with two men aboard waving, rather they were signaling. Bob spotted it while Steve and Lacey were planning a short stay in town. He continued to observe without mentioning it and then decided that these guys were in need of help. He turned the yacht in their direction and asked Lacey to go below until he could determine if they were legitimate or not.

"Ahoy," Bob shouted forming his hands around his mouth as he neared their silent vessel. "What's the problem?"

"Ahoy," the taller one yelled back, "We're out of gas. Can you help us?"

Bob had plenty of fuel to spare and could easily hand them a tank, but he wasn't sure, and he said to Steve, "What do you make of it? Do these guys look OK to you?"

"There's no way to tell. You can pull over there if you like, but I've got a pistol below; I think I'll get it." Steve remarked and headed down the steps, toward the front of the boat, through the galley to his cabin. His bed was still unmade with the sheets and bedspread in a pile.

His knapsack was sitting on one of the two bunks, and he reached in it and dragged his hand along the bottom beneath his clean socks and underwear until he touched the cool steel of his .38 caliber Smith & Wesson. It felt heavy and solid in his hand. He mashed a full clip of ammo into the handle, stuck two more clips into his pant pockets and headed back to the galley to the stairwell and up to the deck.

Captain Bob hadn't moved and continued to keep the Bobbie Magill several feet away from the stranded boat and then moved in closer. As the two boats neared each other one of the men in the other boat tossed a line to Steve. Bob cut the engine, and the two boats came together. Then suddenly the two strangers reached under a sheet of canvas, withdrew a shotgun each, and pointed them at Bob and Steve.

One of the thugs yelled out, "Put your hands behind your head and lie down on the deck!"

Steve went down trying to lie at such an angle that they couldn't see the pistol in his hand. Bob wasn't used to taking orders, not even from two thugs pointing shotguns at him, and he remained standing and glared back at the two. The thought occurred to him that the two brigands stood so close to each other that he might be able to take advantage of them. He shouted back, "You two are really stupid!" Then in a flash, he leaped at them, his left arm around one and his right arm around the other, the three of them tumbling onto the deck. Both shotguns roared, but at such an angle, that no one was hit except for the Bobbie Magill, leaving two giant holes, one in the side of Bob and Lacey's cabin and the other though a window in the galley.

Steve jumped up, leaped across the gunnels of the fishing boat and pressed his pistol against the head of the first thug and ordered, "Drop your weapons or I'll blow his brains out!"

Lacey had been in her cabin when the blast ripped through the cabin wall, across the foot of her bed and into the opposite wall. Terrified that more blasts might follow, she rolled onto the floor then crawled out to the galley, where she saw the destruction from the second discharge. Peeking out one of the windows, she could see that Bob and Steve had taken control.

Lying on the deck of the pirate ship was a roll of duct tape, probably intended for the three of them, but the tables had turned. Bob reached down, picked it up, began wrapping the wrists and ankles of each of the two bandits, and proceeded to secure them to the boat railing.

Lacey finally made it to the deck relieved to see that Bob and Steve were in control. "What ever are we going to do with these two and that boat of theirs?" she called out to Bob.

"The Coast Guard will have to take possession of these pathetic crooks and their boat; otherwise, I'd just torch it, with them in it. That was very stupid of them to stand together like that. They should have been spread out. I couldn't have taken them if they had."

Bob then went down to the galley, popped the top off of a Sierra Nevada, made the call to the Coast Guard and then proceeded on course towards Santa Barbara, with the pirate boat in tow.

As it began to get dark, they met up with Petty Officer Gonzales, not far from Point Argüelles, and Bob surrendered the two pirates and their boat.

The Bobbie Magill continued sailing through the night and early morning past Point Argüelles and then headed east, past Point Conception, into the Santa Barbara Channel. It was a full moonlit night and they were able to see the Channel Islands to the starboard side and the coastal surf and the Santa Ynez Mountains off the port side.

Captain Bob guided the boat dangerously close to shore in order to see the 'glowing tides' that were crashing onto the rocky beach. (This bioluminescence frequently would occur when there were large amounts of phytoplankton brought up to the surface, causing the white water part of the wave to glow brightly.)

Before the sun arose, they pulled in to the harbor, dropped anchor, went to bed and slept through the morning almost until noon.

Steve awoke, sat up, rubbed his eyes, stretched, looked around the cabin and realized that he had slept for almost nine hours straight. He walked to the head, threw some water on his face, brushed his teeth and then returned to the cabin.

The few days at sea had been a terrific adventure and he knew that it was now over. He quickly dressed with a clean set of underwear, Levis and T-shirt and gathered up what few personal items he had laying around the room, including his pistol, and repacked them in his knapsack. He was glad that he had packed the piece, and he was thankful that Petty Officer Gonzales from the Coast Guard hadn't asked if he had a permit to carry it.

The last remaining item was his moon medallion lying on the end table next to the bed. He picked it up, placed it in his pocket and then he headed out. As he walked through the galley he spotted a small amount of coffee remaining in the Mr. Coffee Maker, helped himself to the last cup and then turned the switch to its off position. To his right he saw the large hole that had been blasted open the previous afternoon. There were several pieces of buckshot lying on the counter.

Outside on the deck, Bob and Lacey were drinking coffee together: he in his swim trunks and a bright red-flowered Hawaiian shirt and she in her usual bikini. Steve scanned the landscape: the harbor, Stearns wharf, the palm lined beach, sunbathers, bathers playing volleyball, the store fronts along Cabrillo Boulevard and the Santa Ynez Mountain in the background. There was an access path running along the beach dotted with skaters, joggers, and bicyclists. As he looked out into the channel, he was surprised to see several oilrigs on the horizon.

Standing near the bow, Steve sipped his coffee and continued to regard the scenic beauty of Santa Barbara.

Lacey called out to him, "Steve, you haven't said what you're going to do for sure yet. We would love to have you stay with us."

[80]

"I've really had a good time with you both, and, of course, I'd like to stay. Nevertheless, I need to get back to Big Sur. First, I'd like to call my dad, he lives in Cathedral City, and I'd like to see the Mission before I leave."

Bob responded, "I'm getting hungry; why don't you join us for lunch and then you can take off? If you need a ride to the Mission, I can give you a lift. I'll soon be calling my son Jim to come pick us up."

Santa Barbara is the home of many 'firsts': multiple listings, Lockheed Aircraft, movie studios, one of four sites to start the Internet, Sambo's Restaurants, GOO (Get-Oil-Out) group started to combat Oil Spills. Oprah sold her place in Florida and moved to Santa Barbara. The names in the surrounding vicinity include Michael Jackson's Neverland Ranch, former President Ronald Reagan's ranch, David Crosby, Cheryl Tiegs and Bo Derek.

The best place to go in Santa Barbara is along State Street where there are lots of restaurants, bars and clubs. Sitting at one of these fashionable cafés, sipping lattes and people watching is a fundamental pastime. Most places are expensive, but nobody said paradise was cheap. Santa Barbara, even for being known as an 'old money' town, is very relaxed and friendly. You can dress casual or dressy and Lacey wrapped a sarong around her waist, stepped into her flip-flops and was ready to go.

Steve, Captain Bob and Lacey stepped onto the dock and quickly located a shuttle to take them across Highway 101 to the corner of State Street and Cabrillo.

After walking a few blocks, they decided on lunch at the Cafe Buenos Aires. Their Argentine menu boasted their fantastic Mojitos drink and from the courtyard came some cool sounding South American Smooth Jazz. They were seated in a canvas-covered courtyard with a foundation in the center.

Cigars from Havana

Captain Bob was a gambler, and his gambling debts had escalated over the past few months beyond his ability to cover them. Consequently, he was under the watchful eye of two gangsters by the names of Dollfuss Simpson and Jerry Red Feather.

These two hoodlums worked for Rodger Hightower, a self-made billionaire who had made his first fortune in Silicon Valley creating high-tech startups. He was quite imaginative, and during the high-tech boom of the '90s, the venture capital fellows on San Hill Drive were willing to throw money at anyone that had any resemblance to being the next Steve Jobs.

However, as they say, what goes up must come down, and in 2001, the stock market plunged signaling the end of easy VC money.

Rodger Hightower, in the meantime, along with a shocking number of other valley businesspersons, had accumulated large sums of wealth. In the midst of business closures, the Enron scandal, lost jobs and financial ruin the members of this select club went about unscathed, building large twenty-room mansions in the hillsides, villas in Cabo San Lucas, expensive yachts requiring large crews and staff while looking for other ways to enrich their lives.

Hightower began investing in and importing Cuban cigars. Certain cigars would sell to his highbrow customers for as much as $500 each. Of course, it was illegal to import anything from Cuba. Nevertheless, he had no qualms about it because that enabled him to keep the price high. He had no moral apprehensiveness either since he reasoned that he wasn't a narcotics trafficker. There was no law against cigars, only Cuban cigars. Besides, he believed the US should have resolved its differences with Cuba a long time ago; but since it hadn't, so much the better for him.

The majority of the shipments arrived from Cuba through Mexico and then traveled by either land or water to the US. Pajaro Dunes, near Santa Cruz, was one of the major distribution points. Rodger had a rush order for cigars that needed to go to a customer in Santa Barbara.

Captain Bob owed Rodger several thousand dollars, and Bob was short on cash and requested that he be given an extension on his past due payment. Rodger agreed with the proviso that Bob make a delivery for him. He was to receive the shipment at sea and then deposit it with a location in Santa Barbara still to be determined. The plan was to make it appear as if some wannabe pirates were attacking Bob's sailboat. Bob would overcome the pathetic brigands and, when no one was looking, receive the package of cigars. He could quickly hide it in the on-deck cabinets until it was safe to move it to another location. The plan didn't call for the shotgun blasts that ripped out two holes in the side of his boat, however. Therefore, Bob decided that he was going to hang on to the cigars until some agreement could be worked out regarding his being compensated for the damage to the Bobbie Magill.

After lunch and people watching on State Street, Bob called his son Jim on his cell phone to come and pick up Lacey, Steve and him. They all rode together back to the boat in Jim's Lexus where they picked up their luggage and the package of cigars. Everything was safely stowed in the trunk and backseat, and they all headed up San Ysidro Street to Montecito where the Morrison estate overlooked the beautiful Santa Barbara Channel. The homes on this street were large, expensive and looked beautiful as they approached the drive leading into Captain Bob's manor.

The electronic gates swung open as Jim pushed the remote control on the headliner of his Lexus, pulling forward onto the circular driveway to the front of the modern Spanish styled hacienda and stopping behind a parked older model sedan.

A merger of old and new California, the grounds and buildings spoke of tradition, comfort and wealth. Palm trees, banana trees, and red bougainvillea blooms served to accent the arched windows and orange tiled roof of the low-level adobe brick abode. The park-like setting and grandeur of the place seemed as though staff and servants would greet them, but there were none.

Jim opened the trunk and they each took their own luggage, except Bob carried only his cache of Havana gold leaving his suitcase for Jim.

As Jim reached for his key to open the front door, he noticed that it was unlocked and passed it off because this was probably Reyna's day to clean. Fresh flowers in the entry released a clean fragrance, and the tawny-ocher Mexican tile sparkled from having been recently scrubbed and waxed. The glass from the front windows and the overhead chandelier glistened as the afternoon sunlight emitted a rainbow of colors throughout the room.

Bob showed Steve his room and then led Lacey to the master bedroom where they deposited their baggage and the cigars. He then went to the kitchen and opened for himself a Sierra Nevada Ale, taking a long first gulp.

As he set his bottle on the counter and began to look for a bag of pretzels, in walked Dollfuss and Jerry Red Feather. Jerry Red Feather stood as tall as Bob and a head taller than

Dollfuss. Both wore flowered Hawaiian shirts beneath linen jackets, baggy trousers and leather shoes. Dollfuss wore his hair wet and combed back, whereas Jerry Red Feather wore his shoulder length and dry. Dollfuss was the speaker, and Jerry Red Feather was the enforcer.

Dollfuss spoke first. "Hello, Bob. I believe that we've met before and I think you know my partner here, Jerry Red Feather?"

Bob knew already what was happening and answered, "Yes Dollfuss, how are you? And you, Jerry, it's good to see you. I suppose you're here for the pickup?"

"That's right," Dollfuss replied. "If you'll get it for me, we'll be on our way."

At that moment, Steve had just returned from his room. He headed to the kitchen and soon realized that he was walking in on something. He held back and listened in.

"Dollfuss, I wish you'd have given me a chance to talk with Rodger before showing up here. There's a little matter we need to discuss; it's about the holes in my boat. I believe I'm entitled to some compensation for that."

Dollfuss replied, "Rodger sends his apologies for that unfortunate incident, however, I've been instructed to pick up the parcel that belongs to us; *compris?*"

Calmly, Bob held his position. "Not until we settle the matter of the boat. I'm sure that if I can talk with Rodger, he'll understand the situation."

Bob watched Jerry Red Feather ease forward toward him. "You come any closer and it'll be the last time! Dollfuss, call off your goon. Why? All this over a box of cigars?"

Jerry Red Feather continued forward and Bob took a defensive position: one foot a little forward of the other, slightly clinched fists stacked above belt level. Jerry then threw the first blow, which Bob quickly deflected by raising his arm past his face. Then in one continuous motion, he reached with both hands grabbing Jerry's head, pulling it down while simultaneously raising his knee into his lowered face. Jerry fell back into the wall and Bob pounced.

What followed was a mêlée as the two struggled to gain dominance over the other. Both Dollfuss and Steve watched the fracas, not sure whether to join in or allow it to run its course.

While all this was taking place, Lacey had been taking a shower. She dried off while shaking her head like a puppy out of a swimming pool, sprinkled some powder on her tush, took a quick peek at her boobs while lifting them from underneath a bit, hastily put on a robe and headed toward the kitchen where she heard the uproar and met Steve standing in the hallway. Together they watched the two struggling on the floor.

After a few minutes had passed, Dollfuss pulled out his packed pistol, walked over to the two thrashing about, pointed it directly at Bob and ordered him to stop or he would shoot.

Steve didn't fully understand what he was observing, but he knew that he had seen enough. Dollfuss' back was toward Steve as Steve stepped out from the hallway into the kitchen, quickly creeping up behind him. Steve then reached around and grabbed the pistol in a valiant attempt to disarm him. Steve managed to seize the firearm, but missed Dollfuss, who turned and grabbed his assailant, knocking the pistol to the floor. The two rushed to recover the liberated firearm much like football players scrambling to recover a fumbled football. As the two fought unsuccessfully, Lacey saw her chance, rushed to the scene, and grabbed the gun herself.

Pointing the pistol directly at Dollfuss she shouted, "Stop right now or I'll use this! If you don't believe me, just try me. I don't know what's going on here and I don't care."

The fighting stopped. The four men all gave a look of surprise as they saw Lacey in her robe standing with her legs spread apart and her arms stretched out with both hands on the gun. She pulled the hammer back and waited.

Captain Bob was the first to rise. He walked over to Lacey and reached for the gun. "I'll take that if you don't mind."

Then looking toward Dollfuss and then Jerry Red Feather, Bob said, "Get up and get out of here! This could have been worked out; I hope that it isn't too late."

Dollfuss and Jerry Red Feather both stood and began to walk toward the door. Dollfuss turned while straitening his jacket and warned, "This isn't yet over. When Rodger hears about this incident today, you're going to regret not having handed over the package to me."

After the two gangsters departed, Lacey and Steve waited for an explanation. Bob gave the details about how he owed money to Rodger Hightower and the subsequent plan to deliver the cigars. Bob told them that he was justified in withholding the cigars.

After Steve had heard the entire story, he remarked to Bob' "I think you made a bad decision to withhold the cigars. You already owed him money. Now you owe him money and cigars and we just got the better of his two thugs. Making an issue of who is responsible for the holes in your boat is an irrelevant debate. Take your lumps and quit while you're ahead. These guys are gangsters, and I doubt very much that you'll win in the end. Back in Monterey, Addis Abba and I spent the night in jail because of your mouth. Then back on the boat, you subjected Lacey and me to the wrong end of a shotgun. This is your war, not mine and I don't want any part of it. I just left a war that made no sense to me, and I don't want to participate in another. I need to use your phone; I'm calling a taxi. Lacey, you'd be well-advised to do the same."

The driver of the Yellow Cab pulled up to the front gates and honked his horn. Steve headed to the front door. Bob and Lacey followed. As Steve opened the door, Bob stopped him for a moment. "Steve, you're right about all this. I have created a mess of things. Tomorrow I'll contact Rodger and attempt to straighten it out with him. I'd like to have you stay a little longer. I'm sure I can make this up to you."

"Bob, I'm sorry. I had a great time on the boat in spite of everything. Let me know how things work out."

Return to Big Sur

Steve climbed into the waiting taxi and rode to the Amtrak Station at the corner of State and Yanonali Streets. He bought a ticket for the next train north that was to arrive from Los Angles early the next morning.

With nothing to do, he took the shuttle to Mission Santa Barbara and then returned to State Street and took in a movie. After a late night slice of pizza and a draft beer, he returned to the train station and spent the night on a bench.

The next morning he awoke in time for the train to Salinas. First, he went to the men's room where he washed his hands and face. He then returned with time to spare and purchased a Danish from one of the vending machines positioned along the wall near the door leading to the tracks where he was to board.

Steve climbed the steps into the passenger car and pushed his way inside through the two-way doors. The car seemed almost empty, and he took a seat next to a window. It was quite comfortable, and the entire interior was much more luxurious than he had expected. He sat in a section of seats surrounding a foldaway table that could be either stowed away or left standing. He fussed with it folding it away and then repositioning it.

Out the window, he could see one more passenger running toward the steps of his car. She was struggling, carrying a baby in one arm, a suitcase in the other with a purse strapped to one shoulder and a bag probably full of formula and diapers hanging from the other. He could see her ticket sticking out from the side pocket on her purse.

At the bottom of the steps, she stopped, sat the suitcase on the ground, turned around, placed her hand above her eyes as a sun shield and yelled to the young boy who had obviously fallen behind. "¡Juan, venga! ¡Venga, rápido!"

The young boy slowly caught up to his mother. She helped him up the steps, then picked up the suitcase and pushed her way through the two-way doors, stopping before the section of seats opposite the aisle from Steve.

"Gracias, señor," she remarked as he quickly helped her with her suitcase, placing it in the luggage rack close by.

"De nada, señora," he responded as she placed her remaining two bags on the floor and her baby on the seat next to her. She began immediately removing her baby's diaper. Her young son took the seat across from her and began banging his pudgy hands on the table that separated him from his mother. Looking up at him, she placed her index finger at her lips, gave him a quick "¡Shhhsh!", then looked back down and resumed changing the diaper.

A strong smelling effluvium emanated from the baby's direction. As Steve watched her folding the waste-filled cotton fabric, sealing it with the built-in tape strip, he wondered if she were going to put it into her bag or dispose of it in the bathroom or at least somewhere else. She left it lying on the seat and ensued with further cleaning of the baby's butt with 'wet-ones', then sprinkling it with 'Johnson & Johnson's' baby powder before applying a clean diaper.

Of course, he thought, *it would be a great deal of effort to remove it now. She'll probably take care of it later.* He continued to observe and hoped that she didn't mind his looking her way. She looked up, smiled and returned to her work, dressing the baby. He returned the smile and continued to watch gleefully, enjoying the moment.

"All aboard!" the conductor roared while standing on the bottom step, waving ahead to the engineer. Steve watched him out the window, as moments later, the train began pulling from the station heading west through Santa Barbara and then turning north at Goleta. The conductor stepped inside, pushed his way through the two-way doors, and stopped where Steve was sitting, then asked for his ticket.

Suddenly, Steve couldn't remember where he had last placed it. Frantically, he began tearing through his knapsack opening each of the Velcro sealed packets. Then it occurred to him that he had stuck it into his rear right pocket, and there it was.

The conductor punched his ticket and then moved across the aisle to the señora, who was now nursing her young infant. She seemed less diffident than the conductor, who nervously punched her ticket while turning his head away. Her baby fell asleep while nursing, and the young mother re-buttoned herself and continued to hold the infant in her arms.

Steve looked toward her and asked, "How old is your baby?"

Shrugging her shoulders she replied, "No hablo Ingles."

Steve couldn't speak very much Spanish either, but he was always willing to try: "¿Cuantos anos?" He spoke pointing to the baby, revealing a foolish grin.

"Dos meses," she answered, holding up two fingers.

Steve spoke, "Voy a Monterey. ¿Y usted?

"A Castroville. Mi esposo trabaja allí," she responded.

Steve continued to ask questions, "¿Como se llama?"

"Me llamo Ofilia Garcia Marquez-Oreillano. Mi esposo se llama Raol Oreillano y trabaja en Castroville a pizcar en los campos de alcachofa. Me voy a encontrar con el."

They both smiled and then fell silent, not because they didn't want to talk, rather because of the language difficulty. They did however continue to look at each other, he with a fleeting look at her, and then she peeking back. When she smiled, she revealed both silver and gold in her mouth. He noticed that she was short and solid. He saw that her face was very red and her hair was thick coal black, tied into a single pigtail that ran the length of her back. Her attire was quite colorful, mostly reds, blues, blacks and greens, decorated with beads. She wore moccasins that were brightly ornamented together with leggings beneath her long skirt.

Her young son appeared to be perhaps three of four. He too was short and stocky, red-faced with black hair; however, he was dressed much more simply, in a T-shirt and Levis with tennis shoes.

The younger infant, though, had the strangest ears. Steve hadn't noticed them right away because he was so distracted with the smell of the baby's excrement. Nevertheless, he soon noticed that its ears drooped almost to its shoulders.

They passed by Vandenberg Space Station on the way to Pismo Beach. Large fields of strawberries and grape vines surrounded them as they rode north to San Luis Obispo. Soon, the train chugged up Cuesta Grade and then dropped down, going to the horse ranches and pasturelands of Paso Robles. At Camp Roberts, they entered Monterey County as the train ran alongside the Salinas River. Oil fields gave way to the Valley, one of the richest agricultural areas in California where they passed field after field of broccoli, lettuce, flowers and berries.

The train let them off in Salinas, and from there the Amtrak bus took them past Laguna Seca to the ocean at Monterey

Bay. By 7:15 in the evening they had arrived in the heart of old Monterey, near Fisherman's Wharf.

Señora Oreillano loaded up her bags and children, climbed down the steps to the landing and headed off towards the terminal. Steven wondered how she would ever be able to find her husband somewhere off in the artichoke fields of Castroville? The bus continued in the dark finally arriving at the Big Sur Post Office, where Steve stepped down onto the parking lot.

There were only two cars parked in front of the Deli. It was late, yet there were still a few people in the restaurant. As Steve entered the front door, he saw Sirius and one other employee, but not Moon.

Sirius acknowledged his arrival, "I see you've returned. Moon is at the house, if that's who you're looking for. By the way, the roofing materials arrived yesterday. Are you still on to help?"

"Yes," he answered, "and I'm looking forward to it, pounding with a hammer I mean. It seems like good therapy."

"Therapy?" questioned Sirius, "why do you need therapy?"

Steve really didn't know why he had said that, and he paused for a quick moment trying to think of a response. "It seems to me that pounding could be a process for dissolving deeply embedded energies that hold the energy of emotional frustration in our bodies. Don't you agree?"

Sirius shrugged and spoke, "Moon is at the house. I'll see you in the morning and we can begin hammering out those frustrations."

Unsure whether he needed to knock or simply walk in, Steve rapped lightly on the back door of the house. Starr heard the knock, and came to greet him. "Hello, Steve, I'm so glad you're back. Moon has been anxiously waiting for you, and so has the roof. Won't you come in?" Together they entered the living room, and Starr started to call up the stairs to Moon, and then stopped and asked, "How was your trip?"

"It went quite well, for the most part, that is. I met several interesting people and learned a lot about sailing, which for me was a new experience."

"Well, Steve, you're a guest in our house, and I want you to feel free to come and go to your room as you please. If there's anything that I can do for you, just ask. By the way, have you had anything to eat?"

"Actually," he responded, "I haven't. But I don't want to put you out."

"You aren't. Just go over to the restaurant and have Sirius fix something for you."

"Thank you, I'll do that. But first, I'd like to say hello to Moon."

"She's upstairs, in her room. It's all right to go up and see her, but be sure to knock first."

Steve knocked lightly and Moon opened the door. "Quick! Come in," she spoke grabbing him by the arm, pulling him in and shutting the door behind them.

"Welcome back, Steve," she spoke. "I knew you'd come back." She threw her arms loosely around his waist, looked up at his face and smiled. It was a look of wanting to be held and kissed.

"You'll have to tell me all about your adventure. Did you have a good time? What happened? You're all suntanned; was there a lot of sun?" She continued looking at his face, waiting, anticipating.

"Yes. There's so much to tell. You won't believe all that happened. The first night out..."

She interrupted, leaned her head slightly forward, and at a cant, while pulling him closer, she spoke, "Don't I get a kiss?"

Steve wasn't resisting her advances nor was he disinterested, rather he was either dawdling or befuddled. He wanted to hold and kiss her more than anything. Justly, he wasn't sure what he was supposed to do next. When he began answering her questions, he should have been holding and kissing. That is why Moon had to move forward with the initiative when she said, 'Don't I get a kiss?'

What followed wasn't a rabbit-in-the-moon kiss, a friendship kiss. It was a light-my-fire kiss, light at first, almost imperceptible, a kiss of the evening breeze, soon becoming a caress with the lips, a kiss growing with passion, then like oranges kissed by the hot California sun, flamenco dancers with castanets.

Slowly the crescendo of passion slid down its gentle slope like slow moving mud. As they withdrew from each other's arms, they continued to hold hands until Moon pulled away and walked toward the door. She opened it and turned toward him and asked, "Why don't we go see Trudy? She missed you too."

Steve smiled and remarked, "But I'll bet she's not as good a kisser!"

Together they walked down the steps and out the back door to the veranda, where Trudy remained sitting motionless except for the continuous nose wiggle.

"I feel sad that she has to remain cooped up in the cage," Moon confessed as they walked along. "But I guess that the alternative was to turn her loose as soon as she received her splint."

Steve countered, "But then she wouldn't have had a chance against her natural predators, like foxes, even owls and hawks. I think it's best for her this way."

As they approached the cage, Trudy detected their advance and moved to the front. She had fresh straw, water and a bowl of carrots, lettuce, cucumber slices and a piece of a zucchini. Everything was as nice as Moon was able to make it. Moon then released the latch on the cage, reached in, took her out, and held her for a few seconds. After a few strokes, she handed the rabbit to Steve, who began petting her soft fur. He ran his thumbs the length of her long ears and played with her feet, rubbing his fingers between her toes and soft pads.

Steve then handed Trudy back to Moon, and they both took a seat near the edge of the veranda. Moon then asked Steve about his adventure. "So tell me about the trip. This time I really do want to know."

He commenced telling his tale beginning with that first night when they spent the night in jail and then about the storm when Captain Bob had confidence in him to maneuver the boat. Then he told of the ruse to get the cigars aboard, the two hoodlums that came to pick them up at Captain Bob's home in Montecito and the fierce battle that took place.

Moon listened intently, but she said nothing until she returned Trudy back into her cage. Then she asked, "I wonder how long it'll take before we can free her?"

Steve rose from his seat and responded, "I don't know, we'll just have to wait and see; she'll probably tell us."

This time Steve took the initiative, taking her by the hand and pulling her toward him. "I missed you while I was away." He put his arms around her. "When the storm arose, I held the medallion tightly, but it wasn't that moon, it was you that gave me comfort. I felt closeness to you while we were apart just as I now feel that same nearness as we're together."

Moon and Steve walked back to the house, and together they climbed the stairs and walked down the hallway, his room on the left and hers on the right. She opened the door to her room and pulled him with her. For a few seconds they both stood there wordlessly, uncertain, anxious.

As their eyes met, Steve could no longer withhold himself, and he put his arms around her and pressed his lips against hers. For a moment, he sensed not only her willingness to make love with him, but a certain amount of aggressiveness on her part.

Suddenly she stopped and whispered, "There's something that we must talk about." Steve interpreted this to be what he considered normal female hesitation and decided to ignore it. The two continued to kiss, very lightly, almost imperceptibly, occasionally sharing each other's tongue while gently moving their bodies together. With both hands, he reached beneath her blouse and began to grasp her round breasts, and again she whispered, "We can do this, but first you need to know something." He continued what he was doing, gently, with increasing passion until Moon pulled her hair back, and exposed her ears.

"Stop! Look at me Steven. I want you more than anything, but not until you see what you're getting."

Hidden behind her long, thick hair were large ears, which hung down touching her shoulders and appeared as if they had been clipped from a baby elephant, and fastened to the sides of her head.

Steve should have been shocked by this bizarre event, but his passion had reached critical mass. Nothing short of a stick of dynamite could knock him off this train track, and he continued to caress and woo her into her own state of amorous frenzy.

Gently pressing her downward, the two folded together onto her bed. The emotion continued to escalate as he fondled her between her legs while mouthing her erected nipples. As her excitement increased, her ears began to grow, larger and larger as if they had been a couple of balloons waiting to be filled, not with air, but engorged with blood, much the same as his penis. As the tension increased, so did the size of her ears until they were fully inflated, looking like wings on the side of her head.

Occasionally he would look up, observe her beauty, her entirety and then return to what the two of them were doing, sporadically falling asleep and then reawakening to resume where they had left off. At times, he would imagine that they were sailing on a blanket of wind in the upper reaches of the atmosphere, among the clouds and upward to the stars.

Totally exhausted and spent, they laid together without speaking. Her ears gradually deflated to their original natural state. She untangled herself from his arms and then walked to her closet withdrawing a robe for herself and returned to the couch with a blanket that she used for covering his private parts. She then lay back down next to him and fell asleep.

Steve stirred with the morning sun shining in through the easterly window. He was feeling very hungry having not gotten around to having the food that Starr had offered him. Moon was already up, had showered and was in the process of dressing. She was beautiful, even with her strange ears, which she now made no effort to conceal. He thought to himself how strange and wonderful it was to have fallen in love with her; after all, he had rejected other women for conditions much less bizarre.

'If you spend any time with her, you will discover her uniqueness.' That's what Jordan had said back at Cal Poly.

He was certainly right about that. Steve thought to himself.

Moon finished dressing and on the way to the door she called to Steve, "I'm going to get us some coffee, I'll be back in a few minutes. Would you like a cheese Danish?" When she got no response, she stopped, turned and slowly headed back to him. She could see the puzzled look on his face and she knew right away that he needed an explanation. "I'm sure you're wondering about these," she spoke, pulling her hair behind her ears and shoulders.

Steve sat up and glanced at her for a split second, nodded, and spoke, "To be honest, I'm speechless. I have no idea what to say. Please, talk to me about it."

Moon moved closer, sat next to him on the bed, and began her explanation. "When I was younger and in school, they weren't as large as they are now. Kids called me Dumbo. They really couldn't help it: they were just kids. My mother explained it to me that centuries ago, around 1350 BC, there was a goddess named Quilaztli. She had fallen in love with a mortal, had made love with him and became pregnant with his child. Her father, Quetzalcoatl, became so angry that he caused the baby to be born with large ears. Because the mortal was a tribal chief, the line thereafter became associated with royalty. When the Europeans arrived, they thought the children with the large ears were demons and slaughtered as many as they could find. As you can see, they weren't very successful.

"The technical answer isn't a whole lot better. I'm not aware of any accurate diagnosis, but there is a disease called Say's Syndrome that produces large ears. My parents both preferred the mythical explanation. They insisted that I was of royal lineage and should be proud. For the most part, I've come to accept it. In a way, it's no different than any abnormality, except that it's more extreme. I guess all the bald-headed people in the world feel much as I do except that there're a lot more of them to commiserate with each other.

"I have had a difficult time getting or keeping boyfriends; Jordan is a good example. I usually try not to get involved with anyone. The entire time that you were away, I kept telling myself that I wouldn't allow myself to get close, but that isn't always possible. Now, you can get dressed, if you like, and I'll get us some coffee?"

Moon stood and started for the door, and Steve called to her, "Please, wait. I need to know, do you know of any others with the same ears?"

She answered, "The only other living person that I know of is Starr, my mother. I know of no others. Sirius' ears are normal."

Steve stood and started looking for his trousers as he talked. "What if I told you that I know of another person with the same ears, a person I saw only yesterday?" He zipped up his zipper and buttoned the top button.

Turning toward him again, she answered, "I'd say that you're mistaken. That would be almost impossible."

Steve reacted energetically. "Yesterday, while on the train from Santa Barbara, there was a young Indian girl, I think she was Mexican. She was short and stout, red skin tone with black hair, and by her attire, I'd say that she came from some remote region. Except for Pampers and Johnson & Johnson, she appeared untouched by modern civilization. She told me that she was going to meet her husband, who worked in Castroville, picking artichokes. Anyway, as I watched her change her infant's diapers, she removed all his clothing, I could see his ears, and they were just like yours. At the time, I just thought it was some sort of deformity and thought nothing more of it until this morning. When I awoke, I remembered that the baby had ears like yours."

Moon began to shine; she moved closer to him. "I wonder if it's possible. If it were true, then that would mean that there are others. Did the mother have these ears?"

Steve answered, "No, just the baby. The little one had an older brother with pudgy fingers, but his ears were normal."

Moon questioned, "You said that she was going to her husband in Castroville. Do you have a name?"

"Yes, she said her husband's name is Raol Oreillano."

"Is there anything else that you can remember?" she went on.

"No, that is all that she said. She didn't speak English, and I speak very little Spanish."

Moon moved close to him, took hold of his hands, looked directly at him and spoke with conviction, "We must find this Indian girl. Since her husband is probably a migrant worker, he'll be on the move; our best chances of finding her are now. Would you take me to Castroville and help me find her?"

Steve could see the seriousness of Moon's expression. He withdrew his hands from hers and inserted his fingers into her hair, beginning at her temples above her ears, and then reminded her, "Starr and Sirius are expecting me to start on the roof beginning tomorrow. Don't you think we should check with Starr first?"

Pulling away, she took one step toward the door and turned toward him, "The roof can wait; you two can do that anytime. Nevertheless, searching for Señora Oreillano can't wait. We need to find her now, before she's gone!"

Reaching for his hands a second time she asked, "So, would you take me to Castroville?"

Hunger pains in Steve's stomach growled as he felt the intensity of her request. "Of course, my darling. How soon do you want to leave?"

Throwing her arms around him she quickly gave him three quick kisses in rapid succession and thanked him. "I can be ready in a few minutes. I'll meet you down at the restaurant."

Steve's stomach growled again as he watched her rush out the door, her long hair flowing behind her. *How very attractive she is,* he thought to himself. After smearing some Old Spice under his armpits, he threw on a shirt and the rest of his clothes, closed the door behind him, and headed off to let Starr know that the roof was still on hold but not before stopping off at the kitchen for a cheese Danish.

Artichokes & Castroville

Raol Oreillano lay silently on the desert floor next to his brother Lozano, hiding in the ubiquitous sagebrush, trying to quiet his racing heart and heavy breathing. He could hear the barking dogs in the distance as the border patrol paced back and forth along the fence separating Mexico from the United States. The thin sliver of moon overhead, like a thumbnail clipping, provided the cover of darkness making this a good night for crossing the border.

Raol had made this trip once before and knew that if they were caught, it was no big deal; they would merely be turned back. However, it was early March, and they didn't want to miss the beginning of artichoke season in Castroville.

As the distant barking of the dogs faded, the two brothers leaped from their prone positions and dashed to the break in the fence where they had passed through before. However, this time there was no hole; the barrier had been repaired. Thinking that perhaps they were at the wrong spot, they walked to the right and then the left without finding any trace of the loose fencing. There was no time to figure this out; their only option was to scale the eight-foot chain link barrier.

They both wore backpacks each loaded with a change of clothes, a sleeping bag, a toothbrush, water, rice, beans and tortillas, and they tossed them over the fence. Lozano stood on Raol's shoulders, pulled himself up and over, and then dropped to the dusty ground. With no one to give him a boost, Raol felt the sting of his weight pulling against his fingers as he scaled the wire fence, hoisting himself to the top and over.

Once on the other side, they picked up their packs and took off running into the dark night. Without any moonlight, they had decided against attempting to follow the low point in the saddle of the mountain range to the northwest as they had done before; rather, they would take one of the well-worn paths that led north, even though there would be a greater chance of being caught by the border patrol.

It was about fifty kilometers to the Shohono Nation Indian Reservation where Pedro Sanchez would be waiting to pick them up, along with as many as twenty others, all on their way to Castroville to pick artichokes.

The hot months hadn't yet arrived. It was for good reason that the later months were called 'the season of death'. The Border Patrol had reported earlier that forty-three people had died near the California border since the start of the year. In previous years, many illegal immigrants had died crossing the border, usually hit by automobiles at night crossing one of the freeways. Fences, technology and agents had sealed off urban places like San Diego, and now illegal immigrants were forced to cross in more remote inhospitable places. They were dying from the sun, baking on the prickled floor of the desert where ground temperatures reached a hundred and thirty degrees before the first day of summer. They were dying from freezing higher up in the cold rocks of the mountains on moonless nights, from bandits who preyed on them, in cars that broke down on them and from hearts that gave out at a young age.

Raol and Lozano walked quickly sometimes jogging a slow easy pace. The desert was littered with garbage—empty plastic jugs, discarded clothes and toilet paper. They paid close attention to spots that there might be an ambush waiting for them. They were concerned not only about the border patrol but also about others, Mexican as well as gringo, those who knew they were carrying cash to pay for the trip north.

After about two hours, they stopped to catch their breath, drink some water, and to share a cookie. It was a clear cool evening and the sky was full of stars. In the eastern sky, Raol spotted Orion, with its three stars, Las Tres Marias, forming the hunter's belt and pointing downward to Sirius, the brightest star in the sky.

In another two hours, they arrived at a place where several others had stopped and were cooking tortillas over a small Sterno stove. They were mostly men, but there was one woman with two youngsters, who sat silently with their mother. They waited only a few moments when more arrived, all going to different places, and then Raol and Lozano decided to continue.

Eventually they came to a railroad crossing where they found themselves in a dry lakebed. This was a pleasant surprise as the area they were in was depicted as 'mud' on their map. Obviously, the mud had dried up. They made a quick transit of the dry lakebed, but had long since given up on running due to fatigue and sore legs and feet.

Raol's spirit began to flag. Even with Lozano as a companion, he was feeling terribly lonely far away from home in what felt like an unfriendly land. Although they were making good and steady time, they were feeling the effects of fatigue, and they agreed to take a one-hour nap. They pulled off the path where there were some rocks to hide behind and sat down on the desert floor. It was probably around 3:00 A.M., and they were about halfway to the reservation.

Lozano drew some beans and two plastic forks from his pack and offered one to Raol. It was cold now, having been dark for some time. They saw several magnificent falling stars and told stories when Raol came up with the idea of taking turns, each telling about something special in his life.

"Hermano, do you remember the time that someone stole Auntie Margarite's apple pie that was sitting on her window sill?"

Lozano looked at Raol, somewhat puzzled, "Yes, I do."

"Well, it was I that took it. I never told anybody before," Raol confessed.

"I had no idea that it was you. She was mad, mad at everybody. First, she got after Miguelito, and then Maria. Then she blamed Jose and Manuel; then she even blamed me. Why did you do it?"

"When I passed by, it smelled so good and I was hungry. I thought I'd just sneak a piece and leave the rest. However, it was out in the open where everybody could see. So I grabbed the whole pie and ran with it down to the river. I sat there on the riverbank, dug my fingers into the soft warm corn topping and into the apples and spooned several bites into my mouth. It tasted so good! I should have quit, but then I realized that Auntie was going to be mad if I ate a single piece or the whole thing. I dipped in and ate some more and more until the whole pie was gone. I've never told anybody but you my brother."

They each told several stories, and each story was fascinating. "Boring people don't do these things," Raol said. They agreed that whatever was told was said strictly in confidence and that it wouldn't leave the desert. Nothing would be said. Their secrets lay in trust with themselves and the desert night.

Lozano then looked at Raol and said, "Please, tell me something else, please, another story."

Raol paused and thought for a moment while looking up at the stars. He often looked towards Sirius, just below Orion when he was lost in thought. "I was just thinking about what it's going to be like when we get to Castroville. We'll be given a place to stay and food to eat. We'll get up early each day and ride to the fields. It'll be hot and we'll perspire and cuss. We'll be lonely in an unfriendly land and only have each other for company. You and I will be the only ones with these ears, and some will laugh. They don't know that we come from a long line of nobility, of divine origin, from Quetzalcoatl and Quilaztli.

"Nevertheless, we are going to make it. President Bush is going to get a law passed that will provide workers like us with a temporary work visa. We'll be able to be here legally and earn minimum wages. The pay is a fortune compared to what we could make in Mexico, that is, if we had jobs. However, to qualify we have to be here and working, illegally. We can easily earn and save enough to return home, and with what we've saved we can start our own farm. We could raise artichokes, just like in Castroville. We just need to find the right spot, the right weather, and the right soil and with what we'll save, we can do anything."

Lozano had fallen asleep, and Raol eased him down from his sitting, leaning against a rock position. Within seconds, Raol too was fast asleep.

It was a total of about two hours in the bivouac with the wind building and the temperature dropping the entire time. Raol slept well and nearly stayed warm. The night passed and the two brothers slept soundly awaking only a half-hour from sunrise when they quickly repacked what few possession they had removed and returned to the trail.

The next eleven kilometers were flat, open and featureless, punctuated with frustrating loose sand. The sunrise was beautiful and revealed a desert of changing colors. When they reached the end of the loose sand, they knew the next daunting twelve kilometers would be a brutal climb up the mountain to the highest point of the journey at over a thousand meters. It was quite hot now, but Raol and Lozano made excellent progress.

It seemed to take forever to reach the summit. On the way up, they crossed paths with an Indian family headed down the trail, and Raol asked them, "How far to the top?" It was obvious the man's first language wasn't Spanish. He told them there were ten more kilometers from the top. They continued in shocked silence. There was no way it could be ten kilometers; they had already come so far. Lozano resigned to it, but Raol finally spoke up and said, "There is no way it could be ten kilometers to the top!" They surmised the man meant they had gone ten kilometers since the start of the mountain. At least that is what they hoped.

Eventually they came to some power lines and then to the bridge that was to be their checkpoint at the reservation, a desert settlement consisting of one low building, some ruins and a pitiful attempt at cultivation that resulted in little more than a rearrangement of sand. They passed a little Indian boy, nineteen perhaps, selling burritos. He wasn't reveling in the experience at all and seemed to be suffering heavily, his feet a mess and one thigh bandaged.

Pedro arrived around 3:00 P.M. with his truck already half-filled with immigrants with barely enough room for all those that were waiting there at the reservation. Raol and Lozano each paid the two hundred dollars to him and climbed aboard. Pedro managed to get everyone on, however, there was very little room to stand, sit or sleep comfortably.

The truck was an older flatbed cattle truck with side rails very much like those used by the military as troop carriers. The canvas top stretched over a metal framework that was a comfortable height as long as you were seated on the two benches that ran the length of the bed, one on the left and the other on the right. There wasn't enough room for everyone to have a seat on one of the benches so some had to sit on the floor.

Regardless of whether you were on the bench or on the floor, the ride was hard. In addition, the road noise from the roar of the tires and the wind was loud and made it very difficult to talk with one another—they had to shout at each other to be heard. There was the smell of exhaust from the truck and smell of body odor and urine from the number of bodies crammed in to the small space.

Pedro was a nice enough person and he made a comfortable living hauling the workers from the Indian reservation to Castroville. When his truck was filled to capacity, about twenty, he could get $4,000 for the trip. His only expenses were for gas, oil and insurance—what was left over was profit.

One time he had stopped at McDonalds in town to buy hamburgers for everyone. The problem was that all the people had wanted to get out of the truck for some fresh air, and this caused a disruption in the parking lot. Some went this way, and others, that way. Some went to the bathroom, and some went off to smoke.

A local police officer cruising by had stopped and checked for visas, and of course, no one had any. They had all been sent back to Mexico except for Pedro who went to jail.

Nevertheless, he enjoyed very much what he was doing and was content to be providing a valuable service, particularly for the American public in the form of low farm prices. Pedro believed that he contributed to saving a failed system, something that secretly every Congressman and Senator supported. "The work is hard and the pay is poor," he would say. "Americans don't want to do these jobs, but the migrant workers are actually thrilled to have them. For them, the pay is a fortune compared to what they would make in Mexico, and while the work is extremely hard, it's better than no work at all. And, they send a large portion of that money home to support their families in Mexico."

As the sun began to set in the west, Pedro and his current group were more than halfway to where they were going. The highway was but a thin sliver of asphalt running among the Central California vineyards visible in every direction.

Pedro began to feel a pain in his left arm and then he felt it in his chest. He feared something bad was about to happen and pulled over to the side of the road. He was a large man, 'muy grande', he would describe himself. He stopped the truck, put the gearshift lever in neutral and pushed his foot onto the parking brake. He sat there for a few minutes, gasped and then passed away. His large body slumped toward the door, and his eyes remained open wide staring off into nowhere.

One of the men yelled out through an open flap in the canvas, "Hey! What's going on?" There was no response. A second man jumped off the back, walked to the front, and saw Pedro slumped, leaning against the door. He gently opened and reached in pushing against the dead driver to keep him from falling out.

"I think he's dead," the man cried out for the others to hear.

The rest then climbed out from the back and walked to the front to get a look. They began talking softly among themselves. "What are we going to do? What about Pedro; what do we do with him? Does anyone know where we are, where we are going? We can't tell anyone or we'll be deported."

Confusion and fear were the operative words. One man wanted to leave him alongside of the road and continue on to Castroville. A second said that they should take him to a hospital in the next town and leave him there. A third said, "Look around, we're in the middle of a vineyard, let's remain here and go to work." A fourth said, "No, we can't remain here, the grapes won't be ready to harvest until autumn. We have to move on."

Raol stepped forward and volunteered. "With your consent, I'll take the wheel and drive us all to Castroville. I have a Mexican driver's license," reaching for his wallet to offer them proof. "If God is to look down kindly on us, then we can't leave Pedro alongside the road. He wants us to be courageous and do the right thing, and I think the right thing is to leave him somewhere that his family can find him. A hospital in the next town is probably the best place, and safest for us. Does anyone have anything to say?"

A young man in the group yelled out, "What is your name, señor?"

"I'm Raol Garcia Angelito-Oreillano, and this is my brother Lozano. We're from Orejas Grande in the Chiapas Highlands seeking our fortunes in this land like the rest of you, and I now ask for your vote of confidence."

The young man who asked for his name then yelled out again, "I vote for Raol Garcia Angelito-Oreillano and his brother, Lozano." The rest joined in, and that is how it was decided.

Actually, Raol had never driven a truck before, but he got the hang of it quickly, and they were on their way. Poncho Rodriguez was the young boy that had spoken up for Raol earlier, and he spoke a little English, so Raol had him sit in the cab with him and Pedro.

They arrived at Arroyo Grande and inquired where they might find a hospital, and they were directed to the Arroyo Grande Community Hospital. On the way, they decided that it would be best if Raol and Poncho went in together and report that there was a man in their truck that had had a heart attack. Then hopefully someone would come out with a stretcher, take Pedro in, and discover that he was already dead.

The plan went smoothly, until the receiving nurse wanted them to fill out some paper work. They took the forms to the waiting room and pretended to be filling them out. When no one was looking, they sneaked out the revolving door, got into the truck and drove away.

They continued north along Highway 101, past San Luis Obispo, Paso Robles, King City, the small towns of Soledad and Gonzales and at last Salinas. From Salinas, it was only a few miles to Castroville. They had all but made it, and Raol was beginning to feel the nervousness of responsibility.

As they pulled into town, he could see that all the stores were closed except for a few bars. He had been here once before, and he knew that this was definitely a Mexican town, at least at night. Most of the bars had their doors open, and he could easily see inside, the heavy cloud of cigarette smoke, the amber orange light reflecting warmly in the cool dark night, people going in and coming out.

He suddenly felt that it would have been much easier for him and Lozano to go this alone. In his mind, he heard the words, 'He who travels lone, travels farthest.' He pulled on through town, parked the truck and went back to the rear where the men were climbing down, eager to get out and stretch. It had been a very long trip. He let them know that he was going to walk back to the strip where all the bars were to see what he could learn, like for tonight for starters.

Poncho and Raol were quickly becoming friends, and Poncho decided to tag along. The first nightspot was Rosa's Cantina. It was a typical establishment with a long bar, hombres parked on bar stools, leaning on elbows, nursing frosty pints of Mexican beer. As the two walked in, they were greeted with the smells of stale beer, body odor, cigarette smoke and common perfume. At the bar, all eyes were glued on the twenty-year-old television precariously perched on top of an old Frigidaire. The volume was in competition with that of *La Madrugada* blaring from the jukebox. Another fellow was running the pool table while his challenger stood by watching. Along the back wall near the jukebox and the back door, four young girls sat on stools while a fifth sat on the lap of a middle-aged man wearing a cowboy hat and boots. He was working his hand down her backside and into her skirt. She looked as though she was enjoying it. No one else seemed to notice her.

Raol took the only free stool and ordered a glass of beer as Poncho stood nearby and watched. After a few minutes, cheering and applause broke out as the cowboy and the girl left together out the back door.

Raol handed the barkeeper a few pesos and realized that he needed dollars. "You're new in town I see," he remarked and counted out the equivalent amount of pesos needed to equal the price of the two-dollar beer. "You need to change these. Not everybody is as accommodating as I," he continued. "The bank down the street can take care of it for you."

"Thanks for the advice. Maybe you can tell me where I can find work and a place to stay?"

"You'll just have to stop by the fields where you see people and talk to the foreman. If they need help, then you have to sign up, and they'll help you find a place. How many do you have?"

"Oh, just me, Poncho and my brother Lozano," he answered.

"Then if you still can't find anything you'll have to go to the 'waiting place'. That's down at the far end of the street. But, I tell you, be careful there!"

Raol had heard enough. He had been through this before, and it sounded like nothing new. He handed his half-finished glass of beer to Poncho. "Go ahead, finish it," and he headed out the door, back to the truck.

As the others stood around waiting for him to return, they could see his shadow approaching, and they began to gather at the end of the truck. Most of those who were sitting on the curb, stood up, anxious to hear what Raol had to say.

"Hombres, I said that I would get us to Castroville, and here we are. There isn't a whole lot that I can do now. It seems to me that we are all on our own. Tomorrow we'll need to check the fields for work, check with the supervisor. If they need us, they'll sign us up and help us with a place to stay. If that doesn't work then we'll have to hang out at the 'waiting place'. That place is right here where we are standing. In the morning, There'll be others here all waiting for someone to come, someone looking for cheap labor. They'll usually ask for one or two men, not the whole lot. Sometimes maybe it could be everyone would go. However, be aware. Waiting creates tension. Some of them, maybe you, will be drinking, and you don't want to be involved in a fight, especially since most of us are undocumented. So for this night, just try to keep a low profile, get some sleep and then tomorrow we'll look for work. Some of us can stay in the truck and others, if you want, can sleep on the ground. I plan on heading out a piece on this road, to the fields. If you want to follow me, I guess I cannot stop you. We're all adventurers."

Raol found Lozano and told him to get his backpack, that it would be best if the two of them leave now. Raol thought that he could find where he had worked two years before, and they could head in that direction. He had farmed artichokes on the Gibson's Ranch not far from town. There were twelve small shacks on the ranch, each with a wood stove and cold water, and he had shared one of these with three others. They headed out Merritt Street together, into the country, found a nice hidden soft spot, opened their sleeping bags and soon fell asleep.

Raol was taller than most of the other migrants, and he had unusually long ears. Mr. Gibson, *el patron*, remembered that he had been a good worker and hired him right away. Like before, they shared one of the twelve cabins on the ranch. What was different this time was that Mr. Gibson had recently signed a contract with the United Farm Workers, and it was necessary for Raol and Lozano to become union members. This was not such a bad thing because now they would be able to earn minimum wage, be more secure in their work, and receive health benefits. And the most important thing was that Mr. Gibson was able to help them obtain temporary work visas. As a result, Raol was able to obtain a visa for his wife and two sons who had remained in Mexico, and he sent enough money for her to pay for bus and train tickets to Castroville.

Ofilia Oreillano arrived at the bus station in Monterey, and Raol was there with a pickup truck to meet her. Nearly nine months had passed since he had seen his wife and Juan his son. He had never seen Jose his newly born son, now three months old. Raol and Ofilia smiled warmly and rushed to put their arms around each other. Ofilia was so happy that she was unable to keep the tears from running down her red cheeks.

"Ofilia, my dear wife, I've missed you so much. Thank God you've arrived. Let me see my first born, Juan; ¿como estas?"

"¡Muy bien, papa! I missed you so much."

"Oye, how you've grown in such a short amount of time. I believe you're starting to look like a football player—strong legs. And here's the new one, Jose, please, Ofilia, may I hold him? Tell me Ofilia, how was the trip? How did everything go?"

"The trip was long, but it was good. I'm very tired. It was difficult traveling with the two niños."

"Then, let's load up into the truck. We can go straight to the small house that we're sharing with Lozano. He'll be excited to see you too. He's very lonely."

They climbed into the truck while Raol tossed the bags onto the back. It was nighttime, and as they rode through the town of Monterey, she was surprised to see how everything was so alive, with bright lights shining almost everywhere, from dazzling storefront signs and window displays, as well as from the beams of the numerous cars that slowly crawled down Alvarado Street. She could see the townspeople and the tourists out on the sidewalks enjoying themselves. She noticed how differently everyone dressed from each other, some expensively attired and others much more simply.

Raol headed the truck north onto the freeway, and twenty minutes later they arrived in Castroville passing through the downtown. Except for a few bars, the town was dark, quiet. She could see the few hombres standing in the open doorway of Rosa's Cantina; she could hear the music coming from inside as they passed. A large sign spanned the main street that read, 'Castroville, Artichoke Capital of the World'.

There wasn't much more for her to see until they arrived at their small house in the row of cabins on the Gibson Ranch. Lorenzo was waiting for them. He ran out to greet Ofilia and they wrapped their arms around each other. Once inside, she could see that the small room was large enough for a sofa, a wood stove and a sink.

Everything seemed perfect. Coming to California was once an impossible dream, and now here she was. As she looked around, inspecting everything more closely, she could hear the sound of guitars strumming and then singing coming from outside. Several of the neighbors stood at the front singing the way they often did, songs from home, songs of hope, songs of love. As she stood at the door listening, she could see that some had brought food, beans and tortillas and wine, waiting for Raol, Lozano and Ofilia to come outside and join them.

The warm autumn morning sun showed through the windshield intoSteve's eyes as he drove his pickup truck slowly through downtown Castroville passing beneath the large metal sign that spanned the main street while Moon sat gazing both right and left, looking for some indication of where to begin their search for Señor Oreillano. As they reached the far end of town, they came to the 'waiting place' where there was a small crowd of men milling around. Steve pulled his truck alongside the curb and parked. Several of the men rushed to the truck, pushing their way near the doors on each side hoping to be picked for work.

Steve asked if anyone knew Señor Oreillano and received no response. He wasn't sure if the lack of reply was the result of the language barrier or if no one was talking out of fear.

Then Moon stepped out of the truck and pulled her hair back exposing her long ears and asked, "Has anyone seen Señor Oreillano? He has long ears, like this."

Seeing her wing-like appendages, the same person that had befriended Raol months earlier, stepped forward and introduced himself. "I am Poncho Rodriguez and I know the man that I believe you are looking for. He and his brother are working at the Gibson Ranch not too far from here."

Steve stood at her side as Moon rapped on the font door of the small cottage, one of twelve all in a line at the edge of an artichoke field on the Gibson ranch. It had been freshly whitewashed and had a flower box beneath the front window with purple and yellow pansies looking like designer Miwoks smiling at the two.

The door opened slowly causing a squeaking sound and Ofilia peered out. Steve immediately recognized her, stepped forward and hoped that she remembered him. "Buenos tardes, señora."

With a wide grin that revealed her glistening silver and gold teeth, Ofilia quickly returned the salutation and stood there holding the door open while Steve introduced her to Moon. Neither his Spanish nor her English had improved since they had both been on the train from Santa Barbara; so few words were spoken from that point on.

Still holding the spring-loaded screen door open, Ofilia motioned them both inside, directed them to the couch and chair, then brought out two bottles of orange soda from the small half-sized refrigerator, popped the tops, handed a bottle each to Steve and Moon and took the only remaining seat nearby.

She remained sitting quietly as Steve and Moon gazed about the room. The most obvious thing to notice was how compact everything fit into the small area; the equivalent of a tiny studio apartment with living room, kitchen and bedroom all compacted tightly together in a single space. There were only two beds and a crib, so Moon speculated that Raol and Ofilia occupied one and Lorenzo and Juan the other. *How they could have any privacy,* she wondered.

The silence was soon broken when the baby awoke and Ofilia rushed to pick it up. She wrapped the infant in a blanket and walked back with it to where she had been sitting while loosening her dress for it to begin nursing. The infant quickly went for her breast as she resumed her seat.

Moon could easily see the side of the baby's face and its elongated ear and spoke to Ofilia, "Tiene orejas grandes." So as not to seem offensive, she pulled back her hair so as to reveal her own orejas grandes.

Ofilia, expressed complete surprise and exclaimed, "¡Dios mío! Estoy esperando mi esposo; tiene orejas grandes también."

She waited until the baby finished, and then she grabbed her older son, Juan, by the hand and the three of them rushed to the door where she stopped, turned and spoke, "Ya lo versa," and then ran out the door.

Several minutes later, unable to sit still, Moon and Steve stepped out front and sat on the steps. Neither of them had ever seen an artichoke plant up close, so they walked to the edge of the field for a closer examination.

The plants were tall, thistle-like, standing about three to four feet high and about six feet wide. They had a few blue flowers and buds of various maturities. Steve said that he had never eaten one, and Moon explained how they were a very popular item at the deli. They cut the bud in half, steamed and grilled it then served it with a special garlic sauce.

Beneath the low ceiling of fog, they could see the blue-green field of artichokes flowing in all directions, over thousands of acres of rocky soil, up one hill and down another, a sinuous, winding landscape bereft of trees, fencerows or boundary lines, interrupted only by the small row of twelve white cottages and the lane leading to them.

Moon gazed out across the quiet setting and began to question, "I'll bet that you've had lots of girlfriends, haven't you?"

"Oh, not so many; a few."

"Was there ever one that was special, that stood out from all the rest?"

"I guess there was one, but it never seemed to work out." Steve answered, looking down at the ground.

"Why was that?"

"I don't know."

"Was she difficult to get along with?" She probed.

"No, why do you ask?" Steve was starting to get a little uncomfortable with all the questions.

"I was just wondering. Why is it that a man and a woman may seem to get along together and then all of a sudden, it's over, as if it were just a capricious fling, counting for nothing?" Moon lamented as she stared off into the distance.

"I suppose it's like the seed that lands on rocky ground and must survive, being devoured by birds or scorched by the sun, choked by thorns, and pounded by the elements, maturing all along, until that special day."

In the distance, they saw Ofilia walking toward them, with Juan and her baby Jose, together with a man whom they could tell—when he came closer—also had long ears that hung nearly to his shoulders. He was a tall man, not stooped in the manner of many tall men, wearing a western style hat that

made him appear even taller, standing in the full autumn sunshine wrapped in a long-sleeved soiled white cotton shirt, buttoned at his wrists, and baggy trousers, heavily patched with
total disregard for appearance.

Moon took a few steps as if to get a better look at the
only person that she had ever encountered, other than those in
her immediate family, whose unique members resembled hers,
a freakish form explained to her by her mother and grandmother to be a sign of her royal and divine linage.

He was as thin as a hay rake—such slimness tended to
exaggerate the length of his ears and arms. His countenance
was composed of sharp features with eyes that seemed to bulge
from their sockets, yet there was liveliness in his gaze, a fresh
vivacity enhanced by his youthfulness which when focused on
Moon stirred in her a certain romantic desire, a flutter that she
quickly dismissed. Stepping forward a few steps, she was
now directly in front of him smiling and she offered her hand,
while introducing herself.

"Hello, my name is Moon."

"I am Raol Oreillano," he spoke using his recently acquired English while offering his hand in return.

"And this is my friend, Steve. Steve met your wife while
on the train to Monterey. He told me that I might find you
here, in Castroville."

Raol smiled, only understanding that her friend's name
was Steve and none of the rest, and he offered his hand and
spoke, "I am glad to meet you."

Ofilia motioned for them to go inside, so they one by one
climbed the two steps up to the front door and entered the
small cabin, where they began the tedious process of learning
to communicate with each other and sharing their life stories.

Ofilia brought out a photo album that she had carried
with her from Orejas Grande in the Chiapas Highlands containing pictures of their family and the village from where they
had come. She then went about her business, tending to her

children, nursing the baby, serving coffee and then preparing the evening meal of beans, rice and artichokes.

Lorenzo arrived just in time for dinner and because of the small cramped space indoors; they decided to eat, together, on one of the several common picnic tables outside which increased the amount of steps that Ofilia had to take.

As the other workers returned from the fields, they could see that the Oreillanos were entertaining outside, and some of them began to congregate, also, around the picnic tables bringing more food, some cervezas and music. As the twilight sun took its last bow and exited the stage, and the aroma of chorizos and garlic cooking over the open fire filled its vacuum, came the musicians with their guitars, an accordion and singing.

Eventually the festivities stalled, the musicians and neighbors headed off to their cottages and the Oreillanos, Moon and Steve remained alone once again at the picnic table next to the dwindling coals of the fire.

Language seemed no longer to be a barrier as they talked to each other about their family and the story of their ancestors in the Chiapas Highlands, about their quest to earn some money and their desire to return to their homeland. Moon was excited to learn more specifically about what her mother and grandmother had only touched on: the tradition of the Longears.

As the fog sneaked in from the nearby coast replacing the warmth of the dying embers with an evening chill, they returned to the cabin and studied the photographs in the warm light of the only lamp in the room. Raol scratched the names of his mother and father and their address, in Mexico, on a scrap of paper and handed it to Moon. As they adjourned for the evening, Moon and Steve returned to Big Sur ready to make their way to Orejas Grande.

The Chiapas Highlands

The next morning Moon shared with Starr and Sirius the events of the previous day and evening and announced that she and Steve would be leaving.

They caught a plane from Monterey to Los Angeles, Los Angeles to Mexico City, and Mexico City to Tuxtla Gutierrez. There they boarded a train that took them high up into the mountains, through a rugged forest, with breathtaking vistas of the Chiapas Highlands.

The old wooden passenger train slowly gained speed moving up the incline, its wheels gripped tightly to the rails as an eagle clings to its prey. The long thread of passenger cars, led by a steam engine and a coal car, snaked its way along the route, hugging the contour of the mountainside, turning with each curve, weaving in and out.

Moon sat regarding the view as the train arrived at a wooden trestle. As it started across, she looked out the window down at the valley below, uncertain if the structure would hold up long enough for them to reach the other side.

The powerful engine roared as it pulled the massive tonnage up, up the steep incline. They could hear an occasional whistle from the boiler far forward from where they sat. The train gained speed, and they could feel the movement of the coach rocking back and forth, hear the thumping, the clickety-clackety of the wheels battering the steel rails against the wooden ties loosely entrenched in their gravel foundations.

The open windows permitted the warm outside air inside, the only form of air-conditioning. Some passengers stood on the outer steps extending their faces to the passing wind, tightly griping the metal railing, while others remained inside either napping or taking in the vista. In the rear, a man sat with an ice chest selling cold cervezas. There were mothers with children, men playing cards, and a young girl browsing People Magazine. There were bald men, men with hair, and men with moustaches. Some wore soft caps, felt hats, and there were one or two with sombreros. There were fat women, skinny women and no women with moustaches. There were children wearing flip-flops, white cotton shorts and no shirts.

The time seemed to pass slowly, and Moon fell asleep with her head on Steve's shoulder. The sun shown in on the two of them, and beads of perspiration dripped from her forehead onto his T-shirt—he didn't mind at all.

Eventually he noticed there was a cloth shade above the window that he drew downward and snapped securely in place. Even so, it flopped about noisily in the breeze, and he decided just to ignore it. He pulled her closer to him, put his arm around her, and then closed his eyes.

Minutes later, the conductor came by and jostled Steve, wanting to punch their tickets. He held a hole-punch in his left hand, and with his right, he gave Steve a wake-up nudge on the shoulder. Steve reached into his knapsack, removed their tickets, and handed them to the ticket-taker, but he was unable to fall back to sleep. He drank a beer from the man in the rear of the coach, and then another, and another.

At the very back, a narrow louvered door with the letters 'WC' inscribed thereon concealed the water closet. The toilet was nothing more than a wooden box with a pear-shaped hole, the size of a soccer ball, which led straight down to the tracks below. As Steve entered the narrow door, closing it behind him, he realized that in order to keep his balance in the rocking car, he had to keep his legs spread more than normal and keep hold of the wall with one hand while holding his penis with the other. He could see puddles where others before him hadn't been as successful.

As he looked down through the opening, he could see the railroad ties flying past in rapid succession. The motion of the train, the ties rushing by below and the several bruskies made him a little lightheaded and wobbly. After zipping up, he held himself steady with both hands against the walls, remaining there with his arms and legs locked in place and his ruddy visage lowered until another passenger, a small mustachioed hombre in a white guayabera shirt, opened the narrow louvered door and stuck his head in.

"Perdone me la interrupción, pero…,"

"Lo siento, señor," Steve responded and he returned to his seat.

Moon was still asleep. While he remained in the head, she had lain down in a fetal position, filling out the entire bench seat. Steve took the empty seat on the other side, next to the window.

The train had finished crossing the mountain ridge and was now traversing a flat plateau. Jungle vegetation rushed past the window and an occasional branch would brush past or make a scratching sound on the side of the coach. The temperature was getting hotter and the humidity was reaching an uncomfortable level. As the train sped along the countryside, through the small towns and villages, and along the backyards of neighborhoods, there were always children, sometimes entire families standing by watching, waving.

The train slowed, the whistle sounded repeatedly and Moon awoke. They had reached Atototl, and they disembarked carrying everything in their backpacks. From there,

the only transportation to Orejas Grande was bus or burro—
they elected the former.

The bus too (like the train) was quite colorful, with mixed
blotches of reds, purples, yellows and greens beneath a thin,
dried, caked-on veneer of mud. It seemed to them as if they
were walking into a cartoon as Moon looked back over her
shoulder to see if Curious George were lurking somewhere
out there behind a banana tree. The top of the bus was framed
with metal railings restraining several boxes of various sizes
and two cages housing some small scrawny chickens. There
were several five-gallon plastic containers full of water and a
case of Fat Tire Beer from Fort Collins, Colorado. Once inside, it looked much like a 1950s vintage school bus with brown
leatherette seats framed by chrome tubing. Some of the seat-
ing had its stuffing exposed while other seats revealed previous repair jobs that were now coming apart.

The trip hereon was slow going over a bumpy potholed
road with more livestock along its side than people. Had they
taken a burro, the trip wouldn't have been more comfortable
or quicker.

Eventually the bus arrived in Orejas Grande at the center
of town where they disembarked, and the bus continued on its
way without them. From the bus station, they walked through
the center of the small village, eventually found a hotel and
checked into a room on the second floor.

That evening, from their open window while overlooking the street, they were able to see most of the shops and
people, hear the music coming from the cantina below, feel
the wet sticky air that drifted into their room, and smell the
aroma of the iguana cooking over charcoal braziers by the
street vendors. As the night continued on, there were more
and more people coming onto the street until Steve decided
that he and Moon shouldn't remain in their room, rather they
should be experiencing the fete-like atmosphere of the medi-
eval town.

Together they left the hotel and walked along the store-
fronts where there were no fast-food restaurants, no souvenir
shops or franchise department stores; no automobile
dealerships, stock brokerages, or multi-layered parking lots;
no McDonalds, Wendy's, or Carl's Jr's. Instead, there were
simple shops belonging to merchants and artisans: leather
goods, locally made clothing shops, a bakery, and a farmer's
market that covered several blocks. There was a pharmacy
and a Western Union office. Most significant was the fact that
the majority of the people of this community had long ears.

There were several places to eat, Moon and Steve stopped
and sat down at a small outside café. Except for the beers on
the train, neither Steve nor Moon had eaten anything, so they
agreed to share an order of BBQ chicken and vegetables. While
at the restaurant, they were able to get directions to Raol's
home, a few blocks away.

It was getting late, but they started for Raol's house anyway. After all, what else was there to do? There were many
people out, indigenous people going about their lives, many
in traditional dress. Spanish seemed to be a second language
as many remained true to their indigenous culture and tongue.

As they walked by the stores on the cobblestone street, it
became obvious that the local people were extremely good
artisans, very artistic and creative. Moon hoped to be able to
spend some time shopping, especially for handmade items,
unique items and things that she wouldn't be able to get else-
where: reed flutes, hammocks, nets, leather bags, polished and
decorated gourds, clay dolls and necklaces of seeds. The locals were masters at weaving baskets and making toys. Even
though they were at a high altitude, the weather was quite
warm, and it began to rain lightly. No one seemed to mind; it
was only the old man Nojoch-yum chac, the god of rain.

They soon arrived at Raol's home, and they were greeted
by Maria Oreillano, his mother. There were several other
members of the family living there: brothers, sisters, and cous-

ins, all with long ears. Maria brought out the family albums, pictures of the past as well as the present. She told them of a princess that had escaped centuries earlier from the town of Xilonen and had traveled there to Orejas Grande. The town grew with subsequent generations of Longears. The small village prospered during the 1800's due primarily to the success of several local rubber plantations. However, with the advent of synthetic rubbers and newly discovered rubber trees in other parts of the world, many of the rubber plantations were forced to close. Consequently, many lost their jobs.

Steve and Moon were intrigued by the story of the princess. The next morning they took the bus to Xilonen where they met Father Lopez, one of several priests from the Catholic diocese there. He had spent the past several years attempting to organize and index many historical documents and data that were stored and preserved in the church basement, some dating back over several centuries; scanning and copying documents and records into the church's computer.

Father Lopez was aware of the story of the Sainte Bartholomew Day Massacre that had taken place there at Xilonen. The story had caught his attention two or three years earlier when he was sorting documents and noticed that a massacre had taken place there on the same day and date as the famous one in France, August 24, 1572. He needed to pull the files on this event and asked Moon and Steve if they would come back the next day; he hoped that he would have more details for them.

They were given a place to stay for the night there in the church. There were numerous pictures on the wall, which they studied together. It was a simple room with separate beds, which they pushed together.

That night, they went for a walk and had stopped for coffee at a small café when suddenly, from nowhere, there appeared a band of musicians. The music was loud, dominated by rhythmic pounding of drums. Half-naked dancers covered only with loincloth and feathers appeared from the shadows. In their colorful attire, they played and danced traditional folk dances symbolizing fights between bulls and jaguars or between them and the Spanish. Many people gathered around the spectacle until the street was filled to capacity with onlookers joining in the dancing.

Steve and Moon could no longer remain seated, and they too stood and joined in the dance. Gradually the dancers, musicians and the dancing crowd moved on down the street leaving Steve and Moon alone at the café. As the sound of the drums and music disappeared, they could once again hear the quiet noise of the jungle, the birds and monkeys.

Leaving the café, they arrived at a river. It appeared to Steve to be about a hundred yards across where there were several mounds rising out of a grassy plain. There were several long narrow boats resembling canoes resting upside down on wooden racks and one or two tied to the small landing where they were standing.

A young man approached them and asked if they would like to see the alligators. At nighttime, the river was full of caimans. Moon and Steve agreed and they climbed into one of the boats tied at the landing. The guide and a second person climbed in with them, one at the front and the other at the back to operate the Johnson outboard motor and to steer. Not very far from the landing, the man in the front pointed to the shore where hundreds of eyeballs reflected back the light from his powerful flashlight. The banks on both sides of the river were covered with the modern dinosaurs. The driver then pulled in close to the shore and the man in the front dove into the water and began wrestling with a small one. Then to Steve and Moon's surprise, he tossed the small gator into the boat while keeping hold of it around its snout. He then motioned for them to take a picture, but they had left the camera back at their room in the church. They returned to their room and had sex. This time her ears didn't inflate.

The next morning when they awoke, Moon told Steve that she wasn't feeling very well, and they decided that it was probably something that she had eaten or perhaps from the water.

He managed to convince her to take a tour while they waited on Father Lopez and hired the same guide that had taken them out the previous night. This time they went for a ride up the river to fish for piranha. After stopping at the appropriate spot, the guide threw a cow's heart into the river, and their mouths dropped as they watched the carnivores devour it within seconds. Moon vomited.

He then brought out some poles, and they fished for a short time filling their bucket to the top with the reddish orange meat eaters. The guide helped them remove the fishhooks from the tooth filled mouths and dropped each fish into a bucket of water. When they had finished they gave their catch to the guide.

Moon and Steve returned to Father Lopez's cluttered office at the church ready to learn more about the historic Longears. The cleric hadn't yet arrived and they sat down on a long bench that was positioned next to a wall near the large desk. The bench was nothing more than a round log sawed in half, lengthwise, with rectangular blocks of wood nailed at each end acting as supports to keep the log from rolling.

The desk was situated near the only window in the room with the noon light shining in and illuminating the stacks of maps and documents spread across it. There were books piled everywhere. Several old maps were spread across the desk, held open with paperweights at each of their four corners. A wooden crucifix hung on the wall adjacent to the window, and a painting of the image of Christ wearing a crown of thorns hung on the wall above the bench where they sat. In the corner, a small desk stood supporting a vintage IBM computer and printer. On the window ledge, was a large cactus in a clay pot, with a bright yellow bud beginning to open.

After a few minutes, the door opened sounding a low-pitched squeak that increased as the opening widened and ended with a dead sounding thud as the doorknob banged against the adobe wall.

As the lanky priest entered the cluttered room, his long robe created a current of air that ruffled a few of the papers on the desk that weren't weighted in place. He carried a large book bound in old red-dyed leather from which extended several bookmarkers no doubt marking passages that he was prepared to reveal to his guests. Placing the book onto the desk, he opened it to the first marker and took his seat. He took a moment to re-read a small portion from the book and then looked up and toward the two gringos.

"I'm happy to report to you that I was able to locate the record regarding the Sainte Bartholomew Day Massacre, and I have reread the account. I have made a copy of it for you. It is of course written in 16th century Spanish and is not easy to read, even for me. This description was written by Brother Eduardo Guzman who lived in this diocese almost five centuries ago and was responsible for maintaining a daily journal of the events here at the church. Of course, this is only one person's account and we have no corroboration of its accuracy other than by tradition, but Brother Guzman neither spares any of the priests nor makes any apologies for their conduct.

"I had heard the story once before from one of the parishioners here and then the discovery of this record corroborated the account. He told of a clan that had lived and flourished here known as *los Orejas Grandes*, the Longears. They lived together with the Montauks, another tribe. The Longears were tall and had long earlobes that hung almost to their shoulders. They had a reputation of being quite athletic, fast runners and they served as hunters, whereas the Montauks were much darker, shorter and stouter, worked the fields, and picked the fruits of the jungle. The two tribes lived together, but never intermarried.

"When the Spanish invaded the region, they promptly erected a church in the middle of town. I believe that this present church is sitting on the foundations of that first building. They began evangelizing the local citizenry, however, they didn't attempt to remove the local religious framework. Rather, they hoped to merge local tradition together with Roman Catholicism much the same way Constantine organized the church in Rome. They renamed the local deities giving them Christian names, like the Virgin Maria and Sainte Peter, for example. The Montauks seemed to adapt well to this new thinking, but the Longears resisted. The priests and the soldiers had many other problems with the uncooperative Longears. Ultimately, the priests decided among themselves that these long eared savages must be demons and had to be destroyed.

"The priests were unable to establish a plan to deal with these unholy creatures until they discovered that there was to be a wedding. Strangely enough, the wedding was to be between Omecoatl, a princess of the Longears to Xoititle, prince of the Montauks. Never before had this happened, a marriage between the clans. Moreover, because the bride and groom were royalty, a prince and princess no less, this was certain to be a big event. There were to be several days of celebration before and several days following the wedding. The wedding was to take place on the 24th day of August, which coincided with the day of Sainte Bartholomew on the Gregorian calendar.

"There would never be a better opportunity than this with all the Longears at one place at one time and the Spanish bishop began to plan their forthcoming extermination. After making the announcement to the Captain of the Spanish troops, the bishop offered a reward a five gold coins to anyone that would bring to him the gold medallion that would be worn by the Princess Omecoatl at the wedding—the rabbit in the moon.

[131]

"The days leading up to the wedding proceeded with drinking, reveling and carousing. Furthermore, as Omecoatl, whose name was the same as the goddess of fertility, was marrying outside of the clan, it was taken by many that this was the beginning of a new age of the mixing of the clans."

Omecoatl sat at her small dressing table in her second story room, brushing her shiny black hair, parted in the center of her head, hanging down below her shoulders, touching her waist, hiding her long ears, the sign of her family line. When she had finished brushing, she pulled her hair behind her ears and then began to insert several silver earrings, beginning at the top of the lobe and then continuing down to the bottom, eight rings on each ear, totaling her age.

As she looked at herself and her nakedness, she was pleased with what she saw and she hoped that her husband too would find her pleasing.

Through the open window, she could hear the noise and commotion below coming from the street as the wedding guests began to congregate outside her father's home. Some were talking loudly, joking, laughing. It was obvious that many had already had more than enough sangria, this early in the day. Even though her father was the village chief, their home could hardly be called a palace. Nevertheless, it was the only home in the village (except the parish priest's rectory, which was only a few feet down the street) to have a second story.

Today was to be the most promising day of her life. She had saved herself for him; Xoititle, her bridegroom, and tonight she would lay with him in their new home, not far from the edge of the village.

He was nineteen years old, and handsome, the eldest son of the Montauk chief, taller than most of his tribe, standing an inch taller than Omecoatl. He was strong and athletic; he could run as fast as most of the swift Longears. He could sing and play the guitar and fashion verse.

Their parents were excited about the marriage—the clans together would be united, making them stronger and more resilient against the Spanish. She could only thank the gods for the great amount of happiness that she was experiencing. She often wondered how it was that she had been born a princess, from a wealthy family when the rest of the small world that she was aware of seemed to her to be so poor.

As her mother entered the room, Omecoatl felt embarrassed and quickly arose from her seat and covered herself with a cotton sheet that was at the edge of her bed.

"Mother, you startled me," she spoke as her mother reached for her white gown that was hanging from the ceiling chandelier.

"It's time for you to quit looking at yourself and get dressed. The carriages will be here any time to pick us up. Your father is downstairs pacing; I've never seen him so nervous, not even the day that we married. Let me help you now."

Omecoatl's mother was still young and attractive, only thirty-two years, tall and lean with clear bronze skin, round dark eyes and shiny black hair, and most importantly, she had the beautiful long ears of her royal line. She was partially dressed and her hair was fixed, she only needed to put on her mantle, covered with multicolored feathers, and to have her ceremonial headdress placed on her crown. She loved wearing this traditional symbol of office, but it was going to be a hot day—too hot for the regalia, so this would wait until the last moment before climbing into her carriage with the village chief.

At last, mother and her princess daughter walked down the stairs together, arm in arm, each tall and graceful, proud and full of expectation, and joined the many relatives who waited patiently for them at the foot of the stairs. They proceeded out the side door, through the garden to several wait-ing carriages. The caravan moved slowly along the empty village streets in the direction of the river.

The village had been built on the edge of a river and extended both up and down the waterway, but only on one side. Across the way, there were several large mounds on the grassy plains and that was where the gods dwelt. They had entered those knolls centuries earlier and remained there. The only times that anyone other than the shaman priests were permitted to set foot on these sacred plains was during certain religious ceremonies or feasts. This wedding qualified as such a special event and because there were going to be such large numbers of people attending, the frail bridge that connected the two sides had to be rebuilt.

A portion of the lane, extending from the bridge to the tallest center mound, was soft and muddy, so several layers of palm branches, interspersed with banana leaves, were spread about. Across the bridge at the foot of the center mound, a rectangular dais had been constructed with poles at each of its four corners that supported a thatched roof. At the far end of the platform, facing the mounds, there was an altar on which there was positioned an arch with four candles, representing the four gods that sustain the Mayan cosmology. A central flame was to be dedicated to man and god, Mother Earth and cosmos.

Both Longears and Montauks began arriving early in the morning. It was a hot, sultry day and they came dressed lightly, but colorfully. Many dressed traditionally wearing feathers and silver ornaments. Many arrived by water, parking their canoes and watercraft either upstream or downstream, away from the wedding area. Some arrived on foot or by burro. They hung about the village until the priests permitted the crowd to begin their slow ingress over the bridge, onto the sacred land.

By noon, the plains were covered with wedding guests, the Longears on the left of the lane and the Montauks to the right. Some sat on blankets, some on banana leaves, others stood and visited, laughing and having a joyous occasion. Children, some naked and others wearing only loincloths, ran about playfully.

The carriages carrying the bride, her mother, the village chief, and all the many relatives arrived at the river's edge. They all walked across the newly built bridge stopping only to reform and begin the grand procession toward the altar where the groom, his father, the chief of the Montauks, his mother, and the priests and shaman, sat waiting.

As the bridal party began its slow procession the music began to play and a chorus of voices began to chant. The audience all rose to their feet and turned facing the procession.

As the group moved forward, the Spanish archbishop and priests followed close behind stopping several feet away as the bride, her mother, and father climbed onto the dais. The Spanish soldiers crossed the bridge and remained at the back of the audience spreading both to the left and the right.

The ceremony began and the couple gave each other symbolic gifts, the groom giving corn and cacao seeds, and in return, the bride gave tortillas and powder of cacao. Symbolically, this represented the bride turning the raw material given her into food. As the shaman announced to the audience that the two souls were now connected forever, the Catholic archbishop pulled a sword out from beneath his robe and blew a whistle, which was the signal for Captain to begin the massacre.

The assault began as the soldiers circled the Longears and commenced the slaughter. Mothers and fathers made valiant attempts to protect their children, but to no avail as all received the sharp blade of the Spanish swords. Some attempted to run to the river only to be cut down by soldiers on the opposite side. Arms, legs, heads and body parts lay strewn about the holy plains.

When the soldiers had finished the carnage, they built fires and began to burn the so-called demons along with their dead corpses. The rivers were so filled with corpses that for many months no fish were eaten; wolves came down from the hills to feed upon the decaying bodies.

The Princess's gold medallion—the rabbit in the Moon—was never located and the reward was never paid.

The traditional story held that during the melee, one of the shaman priests led the prince and princess down through a hidden opening in one of the sacred mounds to the place where the gods lived, where the deities watched over them until it was safe to escape.

Steve and Moon returned to their room and prepared to return to California. There was a bus going back to Orejas Grande that afternoon and they were on it.

Return to Big Sur - Part II

Except for those first two years while living in the North Country, Sirius Delgado-Light had lived in a household consisting only of his mother, his sister and later, his grandmother. Schooled at home by his mother he never experienced the friendship and style of other boys his age. Early on, he began helping his mother at the deli performing either culinary or domestic chores, cleaning, washing dishes, preparing salads, and mixing salad dressings. Absent a father figure and masculine tradition, Sirius' gender identification leaned, of course, to the feminine. He never assumed the role as head of household, a responsibility often implicit with teenage sons, a position firmly retained by his mother (however, it must be stated boldly that he was not homosexual.) When his male mentor died, Sirius was too young to have retained any memories of him, only the picture of him on his dresser and the lingering tale of how the hunter had been mauled to death by a bear. Then too, his father's own masuline awareness had been watered down during the Viet Nam War, that undeclared conflict that caused countless men to question whether they knew what an adult male really was. If manhood equated with going to war, why then would they want any part of it? Sirius was left with little self-identity.

(At a tender age, when he became aware of the man in the picture of whom he had no recollection, his father, the woodsman, this shaman, this 'wild man,' Sirius locked him in a cage and released the key to Starr. She kept it safely under her pillow lest he be tempted in a moment of weakness to release the monster. Sirius could never gather the daring to ask for it back nor could he muster the courage to sneak it away from her. There was no one to tell him that the secret to his identity remained locked within that cage.)

Starr could simply have hired a roofing company to replace the deli roof; however, the years following Henri's death had passed by rapidly, so fast that she had not had time or inclination to remarry. She was aware that she had failed to provide him with masculine nurturing. It occurred to her that assigning the roofing task to Sirius would be good for him, not that putting a hammer in his hand and sending him off to a lumber yard would make up for those years of masculine famine.

It was in this context that when Steve appeared in her living room that first night, it occurred to Starr that if Steve were to hang around the house for a while, his presence might, in some fashion, contribute in some small way to Sirius' discovery of his masculinity. Steve had been reared by both a mother and a father. Before long, she recognized his maleness, the way he walked, spoke, all his mannerisms; that first evening she learned that he had played football in high school, had served in the infantry, and that her daughter Moon had been immediately attracted to him. She also learned that his father was the sort who got to work early, labored responsibly supporting his wife and children, admired discipline and was able to sit through three services in an unheated church. Placing the two of them on the roof together seemed appropriate.

Steve awakened to the sound of hammering. It was Sirius working on the deli roof. He had finally given up on Steve helping him with the project and started work several days earlier while Steve and Moon were in Mexico.

Steve dressed, grabbed a Danish from the deli and climbed up the ladder to the spot where Sirius was stuffing his mouth with nails while balancing himself on the 4 X 12 pitch roof of the family business.

Steve and Sirius were sitting on the slippery roof pounding nails into the heavy shake shingles when the purple Pontiac pulled into the parking lot. Steve didn't recognize the middle-aged man sitting behind the steering wheel, but there was no mistaking the attractive young passenger. It was Trudy Mills, his former on and off girlfriend from Indiana. Sirius continued pounding, and the racket caused her to look up as she was climbing out of the car. Upon seeing and recognizing Steve, she called up to him. The surprise and resulting distraction caused Steve to miss the nail he was pounding, and he hit his thumb. While shaking his wounded double-phalange digit, he didn't know what to do other than to respond, "Hello, Trudy, what brings you to Big Sur? Hold on, I'll be right down."

Steve climbed down the ladder as Sirius watched wondering at the same time if Steve was *ever* going to be of any help.

"Hello, Trudy, what brings you to Big Sur?" He spoke while brushing the dust from his Levis.

"I'm on my way to Santa Barbara. I have a cousin who's getting married. I want you to meet my fiancé. Steve, this is Fred Saladburger; Fred this is Steve Franks. Steve and I had a close friendship a long time ago."

A long time ago? I don't think so. Steve thought to himself. *It was more like only a couple of years ago. I suppose that would qualify as a long time ago.*

Steve had met Trudy while he was in high school. He was a junior at Richburg High, and she was a freshman at Marston, the county's seat. For a long time Marston was only twice the size of Richburg and had many things Richburg didn't have such as a this, a that and a whatever, but then the Honda Plant opened in Marston, the town morphed into a city overnight. Richburg used to have much more going on, but after the shopping malls and Wal-Mart opened in nearby Delaware, the small stores and shops such as Newman's Meat Market, the Bun's Bakery and Livingston's Department Store slowly disappeared one by one. What remained was a wide empty street lined with vacant opportunities with either 'for sale' or 'for lease' signs in most of the windows.

To many who had lived there a long time, it all happened gradually. Unaware that each trip to Delaware meant another nail in the proverbial coffin for the small town, they scarcely noticed that it had taken on the look of a deserted ghost town.

Steve started this small musical group called 'Steve and the Nomads' and was looking for a gig, a place to play, and he found it in nearby Marston. Once about every other weekend he was able to line up either a school dance or a party at someone's house. These were never financial opportunities. These performances endured strictly for the love of the art or the attention that it brought to him, not necessarily in that order.

It was at one such school dance that Steve saw Trudy. She was pretty and neat and wore her hair piled high on her head with a blue bow. She spent the evening with a friend seated near the platform. He noticed that she was continuously watching him, even when she was dancing, so when he was finished for the night, he approached her and invited her out for coffee.

Steve offered his hand to Fred together with a perfunctory gesture. The two men exchanged handshakes then Trudy remarked to Steve, "The last time I heard from you, you were in Texas. Then I heard you had gone to Iraq. So, what are you doing here, working on that roof?"

"It's a long story," Steve replied and then he changed the subject. "Did you stop for lunch? If so, you might try the crab cakes, they're excellent."

Moon stepped out from the deli to see how Steve and Sirius were doing on the roof and was surprised to see Steve in the parking lot talking with what appeared to be a luncheon guest. Steve called her over to meet Trudy and Fred.

"Moon, I would like you to meet my friend Trudy from Indiana and her fiancé, Fred." Then turning to Trudy, he introduced her to Moon.

Moon was stunned. "Trudy?" she thought to herself, "What a coincidence!"

Steve knew immediately what Moon was thinking. Then while looking at Moon he went on, "Trudy is going to Santa Barbara to her cousin's wedding, and by pure chance, she stopped here for lunch."

Moon remarked, "That's interesting, we received an invitation last week while we were out of the country, from Santa Barbara. Steve, your sailing friend, Bob Morrison is getting married to Ms Lacey Cupertino. I just opened the invitation early this morning."

"That is interesting," remarked Trudy, "That's the same wedding that we're going to. Lacey is my cousin!"

Then Moon volunteered, "Why don't we all go in and have lunch together, and we can discuss it. This seems like it's beginning to turn into an occasion."

Sirius came down from the roof and hung the 'closed' sign in the deli window; Starr came from the house. Starr made up a table on the veranda, set the plates and silverware, water goblets, and wine glasses in place. Sirius shucked two-dozen Blue Point oysters and prepared them on the half shell with white truffle cream sauce and Beluga caviar. Simultaneously he prepared St. Croix crab cakes, with fruit salsa and lime aioli and a plate of Brie with sun-dried tomatoes belden. Then he created a Mandarin oriental chicken salad. Moon opened several bottles of Edna Valley Vineyards, 'Paragon', a buttery chardonnay from San Luis Obispo and placed the bottles in ice buckets along the table.

While all the preparations were taking place, Steve went with Trudy and Fred for a walk along the beach.

Moon, meanwhile, was fuming, first because Steve was walking on the beach with Trudy and secondly because she had unnecessarily created this afternoon extravaganza without having first thought it through. Now, she was stuck with it.

The three removed their shoes and climbed down the rocks to the beach. The tide was out and the beach was extra deep with smooth dry sand. There were lots of sand flies hovering over the shore, and a portion of the carcass of the dead sea lion that had been there for some time still left its offensive smell.

Fred sat on a rock while Trudy and Steve continued to walk. Trudy wanted to know, "It seems like you and Moon are together?"

Steve slowly responded, carefully wording his reply. "I've only known Moon for a short time. What about you and Fred? He seems like a nice enough guy."

"We've been going together for almost a year now. Does that mean that there's no chance for us any more?"

"Probably not." After a pause he continued. "We've had so many chances to make it work, and then something comes along and spoils it. Nevertheless I do think of you, sometimes."

Steve reached down, picked up a sand dollar and handed it to her. "Since I've been here, I've learned that sand dollars, like the sea urchin, have no arms or legs but move around by tiny spines on their body. They usually lie buried under a layer of sand. If it's alive, it'll appear to have a layer of very fine hair on its body not like this one. I guess that it's time for us to head back to the veranda."

Fred had already returned to the deli and was out of sight, perhaps having a smoke. Steve and Trudy returned to the rocks where they had previously descended and began to climb the crag up to where the luncheon was about to begin. Trudy took his hand as she began to lose her sense of balance. Having regained her steadiness she turned toward him and pressed her lips against his, one final attempt at the only man to whom she had ever been attracted. Steve remained fixed, without any emotion, returned the kiss, and pulled away.

At the top of the cliff, they walked single file following the short trail through the ice plant back to the veranda. As Trudy stepped up to the deck she saw the rabbit cage, and excitedly exclaimed, "Oh, look! A bunny; it's so cute. May I pet it?"

Steve shook his head. "It has a broken leg. Several weeks ago, I hit it while driving in the fog. As soon as it heals, I'll be turning it lose. It seems to be coming along quite well."

Moon stepped out the door onto the deck, saw the two admiring the lagomorph, and couldn't resist joining into the conversation. Looking directly at Trudy she smiled and remarked, "I'll bet you'll never guess the name of this furry little friend of Steve's?"

"Why no," she answered, "do tell."

With all the food, water and wine on the table, Starr Light sat at its head and Sirius at its foot, Moon and Steve on one side and Trudy and Fred, opposite. Starr asked that they all hold hands and she gave a short secular prayer of thanks for the food and the fellowship that was before them.

When she finished she expected to see smiles and happy faces on her children and guests, all anxious to dive into the light but festive banquet that she and Sirius had just finished preparing. What she saw were five dour faces each starring downward, none seeming to be interested in the glorious afternoon spread. Sirius looked up at her and shrugged his shoulders.

"Let's eat!" Starr spoke, pretending to be enthusiastic while reaching for one of the bottles of wine nearest her. "Moon, help yourself to some oysters and then pass them around. These are very fresh, we just received them today, and Sirius has just finished shucking them." Sirius looked at his bandaged hand where he had accidentally stabbed himself in the process. Moon reached for the platter, removed one of the grayish calcareous mollusks, placed it onto her plate, and then passed it on without looking at Steve sitting beside her. She then helped herself to some of the white truffle cream sauce and a small sample of the Beluga caviar.

Straitlaced Trudy had never developed a taste for caviar or oysters and she was squeamish about the notion of having to place either item into her mouth. Had this occasion been higher on the Richter scale of social endeavors or if Steve had responded more favorably to her amorous advances on the beach, she would have no doubt been more inclined to bite the mullet. Furthermore, given the sudden unfriendly atmosphere, she was motivated to help herself quickly to the crab cakes in order to avoid having to admit her gastronomic paucity. Fred quickly downed two glasses of chardonnay and then covered his plate with the salad, taking more than his proportional share.

Steve, more than anyone present, wanted all of this hard-faced gloominess to somehow take a drink of wine and lighten up. He had no opinions or feelings about Fred except that he appeared as an unabashed cuckold, nor did he know much about Sirius whom he was still unable to get to know.

Steve just wanted everyone to get along. Moon, Starr and Trudy were the women in his life at his moment, in that order and he cared deeply about each of them, in different ways, of course.

Feeling the call to duty, he dove aggressively into each platter, bowl, dish and container, piling his plate high with the freshly shucked Blue Points, the St. Croix crab cakes, with fruit salsa and lime aioli, the brie with sun-dried tomatoes belden and the Mandarin oriental chicken salad. He took on atypical characteristics he rarely employed such as humor, joking, impishly asking questions of others, and calling each person by name almost to the point of hyperbole. "I could eat a million of these!" When the wine was gone, he asked for more.

Eventually the mood at the table began to change. Trudy and Moon began speaking to each other, even appearing to enjoy each other. Sirius attempted to communicate with Fred, who continuously stepped away from the table for a smoke while Starr and Steve paired off in the kitchen and talked about what it was like to live in Canada a decade and a half ago.

Steve returned to the table and reminded everyone that they hadn't yet discussed Bob and Lacey's wedding. Since Sirius didn't know Bob or Lacey, and wasn't invited, he returned to the roof to hammer down some more shingles.

They decided that they would all go to the wedding together. The next morning Trudy and Moon climbed into the backseat of the purple Pontiac, Fred sat in the driver's seat and Steve took the front passenger seat. It was a sunny day, so they decided to go à la cabriolet. The two women in the back had to wear scarves to keep the wind from blowing their hair.

When they arrived at Bob's house in Santa Barbara, they were surprised to learn that Addis Abba was already there, and the real surprise was that he had brought Havana Charpantier with him as his guest. Addis Abba had come across Havana one day while shopping at the Safeway store in San Luis Obispo, and they had begun seeing each other.

The guests were greeted, one by one, by Bob's son Jim, who helped everyone find their respective rooms. After being settled, all the visitors met with Bob and Lacey out at the swimming pool and spent the afternoon sunning, playing water polo, drinking caipirinhas and mojitos, laughing and sharing stories about the great sailing trip from Monterey.

It was suggested that since there had been no bachelor party for Bob that the guys should load up in the purple Pontiac and drive to Tijuana for the night. Lacey thought it was a bad idea. For one, it was too far to drive, spend the night and be back for the wedding the next day. Second, it was a little late for Bob to be having a bachelor's party since he had been married so many times before. Third, since Bob was a Toyota dealer it would seem a little inappropriate for them to be driving down in a purple Pontiac.

As an alternative, Bob thought that they could instead go to the Café Tijuana, off State Street. They could go in his Rolls, and Jim could be the designated driver. Steve and Addis Abba both looked at each other remembering the last time they went out with Bob at Fisherman's Wharf in Monterey.

It was settled. At around 10:00 that night, the four men piled into the Rolls, with Jim driving, and headed to State Street, where Jim let them off at the Café Buenos Aires. From there they traveled on foot two streets over in the direction of the Café Tijuana.

As they approached, they could hear the sound of the mariachis: brilliant sounding trumpets, the guitarro, the vihuelas, the shifting between syncopation and on-beat rhythm, the heart and soul of Mexico.

As they entered the front door, they were welcomed by the direct blast of the mariachis, the strobe lights and the smaller beams that rotated from red, to blue, green and yellow. The place was packed and there was a line of people ahead of them waiting to be seated. Over their heads, not too far off, Bob could see a nude pole dancer and scantily clad servers carrying small round trays with drinks. With so many ahead of them, Bob handed the maitre d' a fifty-dollar bill, and they were quickly escorted to a spot not far from the stage where they were able to get a good view and order a pitcher of caipirinhas.

Pitcher by pitcher, the evening passed. They laughed, applauded, toasted Bob and Lacey, and paid a lap dancer to visit Bob. With each pitcher, their server accepted graciously a five or a ten and confirmed her appreciation by exposing her breasts, which resulted in roaring laughter, applause and her prompt return each time their pitcher ran low.

It seemed to both Steve and Addis Abba that the evening was going without a snag and that they were going to make it back to Bob's house without any problems. They had only a half-hour before closing time when Bob and Steve both recognized the two men standing at their table wearing flowered Hawaiian shirts beneath linen jackets, baggy trousers and leather shoes. It was Dollfuss and Jerry Red Feather.

Bob acknowledged them both by standing and offering his hand. "This is my bachelor party tonight. Tomorrow I'm getting married. So, why don't you pull up a couple of chairs and join us. No hard feelings, you guys, heh?"

Dollfuss, who was always the talker ignored his outstretched hand, "You gentlemen seem to think that I have forgotten the disrespect that you showed us last month. You may have settled with Rodger Hightower, but you haven't settled with me. I'm warning you, Morrison, you haven't heard the end of this."

Bob was always like a bottle of warm champagne and it never took much shaking to loosen his cork. "I just offered my hand to you wiseass and you still want to take a poke at me. Well, have at it mister, let's just square off now you gutless coward!"

Jerry Red Feather stepped forward and threw the first punch and the fight commenced. Bob threw Jerry Red Feather onto the table and began pounding on him. In no time, the in-house security pulled Bob off Jerry Red Feather and hand-cuffed the two of them. They both found themselves in the paddy wagon of the Santa Barbara Police and on their way to the city jail.

Steve called the house for Jim to come and pick up Fred, Steve and Addis Abba. When they arrived at the house, they recanted the evening's events to Lacey, of course leaving out the part about the lap dancing. They explained that Dollfuss and Jerry Red Feather had arrived and started the fight. The problem was that there was going to be a wedding and the groom was now in jail.

The next morning, Steve and Jim went to the police station to see what they could do about getting Bob released in time for the wedding, which was scheduled to take place at 11:00 AM.

At 10:30, the bride and all the guests had arrived, or were arriving, at the church and Bob was still not out. Tensions grew. The minister shook his head in disbelief. The guests had little or no idea of the problem and listened patiently to the organ music. At 11:15, they began to squirm in their seats wondering why the service wasn't yet under way. By 11:30, the minister reported to the bride that there was another ceremony scheduled for 1:00 and they should consider canceling the wedding.

At 11:45, Steve and Bob arrived, however, Bob was un-shaven, reeked of alcohol and was still wearing his wrinkled clothes from the previous night's revelry. Jim was the best man and he led Bob to the minister's office where his tuxedo was waiting. At last, the bride and groom stood in the ante-room waiting to join in the procession toward the altar as the organ player played Pachelbel's Canon in D major.

It was really no surprise to Moon; she knew ahead of time that she would be the one to catch the bouquet and she did.

Bob and Lacey climbed into the Rolls and Jim drove them to the wharf, where they boarded the Bobbie Magill and sailed off to Acapulco. Addis Abba and Havana caught the train to San Luis Obispo and Fred, Trudy, Steve and Moon turned the purple Pontiac north on Highway 101, with the convertible top comfortably closed.

When they arrived at the Big Sur Deli late in the evening, Sirius was climbing down the ladder from the roof, finished for the day. Starr ended her last reading for the day and hung out her closed sign. Trudy the rabbit waited patiently for her leg to heal.

The next morning Moon sat at her vanity. She was examining her body, her stomach, and her breasts. She was now certain; she was pregnant. Starr had explained it all to her when she was around thirteen, when she had had her first period. Her mother had explained how her ears had twice become engorged: first on the night that she mounted Henri as he slept and the second time when Moon was conceived. Even though she had had sex many times before and after, those were the only two eventful times.

Because all that had been described by her mother did in fact happen to Moon that first night, she suspected that she must have conceived; but she wanted to wait, to be sure. Now she was convinced. This matter was important enough to require thought and attention; Steve had to know, and she had to tell him.

As she dressed, she began to wonder how he would react. Would he want to commit to a lifelong relationship with her, someone he barely knew, someone quite strange to the normal world, someone that might produce a strange looking child? He might insist that she have an abortion. It might be simpler to let him go and not tell him. The baby could grow up here the same as her mother and brother. People here had become used to their strangeness. Raol and his family now lived a few miles away in Castroville. Who knows, there might even be others.

Moon thought about what it would be like on their wedding day. They could say their vows on the beach. They could invite Bob and lacey, Havana and Addis Abba, Trudy and Fred, Raol and Ofilia, and Jordan. *Oh how much I miss Jordan,* she thought to herself. *I wonder if he would come. The ears were too much for him to accept. If it weren't for my ears, we would probably have been married already. I would probably have been at Cal Poly with him, studying modern dance. That's what I always wanted.*

```
HOME
SWEET
HOME
```

A House Is Not a Home

Steve turned right, out of the parking lot of the Big Sur
Deli onto the Coastal Highway toward San Luis Obispo, pass-
ing through the Santa Lucia Range of the Los Padres National
Forest.

The morning fog remained occupied, doing pushups
against the asphalt highway, unable to lift itself completely
out of bed. Big Sur's allotment of sunshine was locked in a
vault at the Bank of Monterey and the coastal community had
to live off the interest. Through the thick haze, he could
scarcely see the ocean below to his right. (The fog reminded
him of that first night when his truck had bumped into Trudy
the rabbit.)

The gloomy crack-of-dawn sun to his left, also known as
the quarterly interest payment, slowly snuck up the eastern
side of Junipero Serra Peak on tippy toes trying to hide from
anyone that might be looking. Through the open window of
his pickup he could smell the freshness of the unfolding day,
the smell of moss on pine-needles, the smell of the fir trees,
the spruce, the eucalyptus, and perhaps even a little of the Old
Spice from the medicine cabinet. From his radio, tuned to
KWAV, the singular warble of Neil Young seemed to falter as

the less than muffled roar of his Ford engine echoed off the nearby granite rock face. The cool breeze coming in from the open windows was perhaps a little too cool for him, having worn only a T-shirt and no jacket. He felt a shiver as the fine red hair on his arms stood at attention waving in the breeze like flagpoles rising out of his goose bumps.

Steve had all day to arrive at Cathedral City and wasn't in any particular rush to get there. Moon had packed him a breakfast of sopes filled with beans, epazote, cheese, and fried plantain and a fourteen-ounce thermos cup of Amaretto Supreme coffee that he held between his legs to keep it from tumbling. He left the sopes on the seat next to him for later.

Steve was on his way to visit his father, but he wasn't going home—that was in Indiana. As he thought about it, Indiana was no longer his home—he had no home. He had left home, given it up and he had sworn that he would never return. Home was once a wonderful place. He had had friends there in Richburg and there were family picnics with Mom and Dad, Grandma and Grandpa, all the aunts and uncles and cousins. He played sports, football and softball and he skated on the frozen lake in the winter. He went to summer camp and sometimes he and his brother would set up a tent in the back yard and cook hot dogs and marshmallows on sticks. In addition, he had his band, 'Steve and the Nomads', the best kick-ass band around. All that was then and it was all in the past, over, done with. He tried putting it out of his mind, not thinking about it. Nevertheless, like a mischievous spirit, his thoughts of home and his mother and father continued to haunt.

At last, the sun lifted its arms, flexing its muscles in unabashed victory over the fog. The morning vapor ran and hid beneath the trees and low-lying vegetation in the Cambrian hillside like Dracula fleeing the darkness.

Feeling hungry, Steve reached for one of the sopes on the seat next to him. Just about the time he finished his morning nibble he came to the road that turned inland, taking him east over the mountain range to the next freeway leading south to the San Gabriel Mountains and then the San Bernardino Mountains to Cathedral City.

The hills were covered, mile after mile with vineyards, as far off as could be seen. Never had he seen so many fields of grapes. The vines all seemed planted, facing south, possibly to maximize the amount of sunlight that fell on the vineyard. Occasionally he would pass a winery with its ubiquitous 'wine tasting' sign.

As the miles blandly passed by, he drifted back into lingering deliberation. Much like Frodo Baggins approaching Mount Doom, Steve crossed the Central Valley heading for Cathedral City. He could feel the weight dragging on him and his mind became wholly consumed by his burden.

Like many mothers, his had doted over him, constantly buying him expensive clothes, making sure his hair was always neatly trimmed, teaching him to play the piano, and bragging about him incessantly to her friends. Their social life was mostly rooted in the church and their family business, a hardware store in downtown Richburg. During his childhood, they had taken several family vacations. Sometimes his mother and father would go off by themselves on vacation leaving a babysitter to watch over the two boys. One time they went on vacation with another couple. Sometimes the four of them would go together, like to the opera in Indianapolis or a Broadway show in New York.

The highway was now a straight seventy mile per hour raceway. Steve held the speedometer to seventy-five and watched cars, trucks and SUVs, alike, all passing him as if it were the Daytona 500. *Did someone change the speed limit and not tell me?* he wondered; *or did they forget to change the road signs?*

He sat up straight, leaning a little closer to the steering wheel as he pushed harder on the accelerator while checking the rear-view mirror for the Highway Patrol. This blatant breaking of the law was something he wasn't accustomed to and it made his heart beat a little faster like a ping-pong ball bounding about the room. He was sure that he was in the flow of traffic with the other vehicles and if he were pulled over, "Well, officer that's my defense!" he reasoned. Remembering that he hadn't had a speeding ticket since he was a teenager, he nervously pushed the button on the cruise control switch, leaned back and took his foot from the accelerator.

As he continued, the vineyards became cotton fields. The white puffs hung heavy in the fields on both sides of the road. Every now and then there would be stacks of bales already picked, wrapped in white plastic, and ready to be loaded for delivery to one of the nearby railroad spurs. In other fields there were ten, twenty, even as many as thirty workers all stooped, picking the threads that might sometime in the near future appear in a T-shirt of his. He gave a childish chuckle as he looked at the broad expanse and pointed to a cotton bush and shouted out the window, "There, that one, hey you cotton ball, you're mine. I'll look for you soon. Don't you go anywhere else, do ya hear?" A worker close to the road looked up from what he was doing, removed his hat and scratched his head as he wondered if Steve were talking to him.

Along the road, not far from the workers were several parked cars, an old repainted school bus with a green plastic outhouse on two wheels ready to be towed off behind it. The porta-potty didn't sit very level, half on the berm and half into the drainage ditch. He tried to imagine what it might be like if someone needed to use it.

Drops of perspiration dripped from his forehead as he came nearer and nearer to his father's home. It was the drama of his last year in high school that oozed from his pores leaving rings of wetness under his arms and around his neck. Unconsciously he rubbed the three-day stubble on his face.

It was during his last year of high school; he had done his best to ignore the rumors of his mother's infidelity. He had been certain that they weren't true yet they continued to reappear. His parents had become good friends with the Bolingbrokes; that is all that it was. He was a prominent businessperson in town, the mayor, no less. It is true that Henry Bolingbroke would sometimes visit his mother at the hardware store. "So what's the big deal?" he would exclaim! It hurt deeply to hear what some of his friends were saying.

Then one night, he was joyriding in a car full of friends. He was in the backseat and they were heading out on a backcountry gravel road when they came upon his mother's car parked alongside of the road. It was dark and difficult to see.

"Hey, isn't that your mom's car?" someone spoke.

The driver slowed to a crawl and Steve forced himself to look. Unable to see through the foggy side window, he slowly cranked it down and took a better glance. Embarrassed, at what he had seen, he quickly ducked down and returned the window to its closed position.

That evening's event and what he thought that he had seen tormented him throughout the days and weeks that followed. Unsure of what he needed to do, he did nothing except try to keep it out of his mind. Nevertheless, the question kept surfacing, 'Why?'

He found it difficult to be around or near his mother and he repeatedly found excuses to avoid her. He began identifying undesirable traits exhibited by his father: not tall enough, antisocial, humorless, boring to be around, a stuff-shirt, and overly religious. On the other hand, Henry Bolingbroke was none of those things; rather he was tall, handsome, outgoing, witty, and always the life of the party. Steve soon took on a disliking of the whole bunch.

As he slipped into melancholy funk his grades worsened, he stayed out later than permitted by his parents, he argued incessantly with his friends and teachers and with his parents, that is if he spoke to them at all. He began smoking and getting drunk on 3.2 beer. Usually the only conversations that took place with his parents were what he perceived as their criticisms of him, lecturing and berating him. It was during one such tongue-lashing from his father that Steve struck back, charging his father that he should pay more attention to his own affairs.

"Hypocrite! Take the log out of your own eye," Steve shouted at him, quoting the Gospel of Mathew.

"How dare you speak to me that way," his father countered. "Who do you think you are, referencing the Lord's word?"

Steve then attempted to explain the rumors that had been going around about his mother and what he had witnessed himself directly that night on the backcountry road. His father called his mother into the room and asked her about what had been levied against her. Following her denials Steve was ordered to retract his accusations and when he refused, he was whipped with a green branch from an elm tree until he bled, first by his father and then by his mother.

He barely noticed the landscape around him as the memory of that day projected painful images on the windshield of his truck: yelling back and forth, his being wrestled to the floor and his shirt ripped from him, the repeated thrashing of the elm branch, the bloody welts across his face and back, screams of "Liar! You take that back, do you hear me?" and finally his running away out the back door of the house."

He was now two hours north of Los Angeles, on a strip of flat yellow earth dotted with sagebrush and California chaparral. Tens of thousands of oil pumps bucked and thumped like squeaky steel horses, above the sun-caked ground, sapping crude from nearly a mile down.

He pulled to the side of the road wondering if he should continue this trip or turn around and return to Big Sur. It all seemed too painful. Slumping in the seat of the truck, he let his legs slide forward as far as they would go beneath the dashboard, past the clutch and brakes, put his head back and closed his eyes attempting to clear his mind. He extended his outstretched arms as if he had just awakened from a deep night's slumber. The outside sounds sneaked in: the thumping and squeaking oil pumps, the mooing of a few cows grazing near the edge of the adjacent paddock, and the whooshing, whining and roaring of the passing cars on the highway, all seemed to serve as a balm to his sorrow. He thought of that moment on the stormy sea as Captain Bob had told him to keep his eye on the compass, not to worry, it was only a squall, and it would soon pass. He remembered how he had held the medallion Moon had given him, the symbol of friendship, and he withdrew it from his pocket and held it tightly in his closed fist.

He knew how much his father had hurt him, yet he knew how much he missed his father, how he wanted to be reconciled with him. There was nothing to be gained by turning back, he reasoned, and there might be a chance of something good happening if he continued. He restarted the engine and pulled back onto the highway toward Cathedral City.

Cathedral City

Steve turned his pickup truck off the Calle de las Palmeras onto the crunch and crackle of the crushed stone and gravel lane leading back to his father's small Silver Stream trailer. The house was sitting on concrete blocks, wheels removed and stacked off to the side. There was no shade, anywhere. Heat waves rippled from the desert floor over the hazy horizon giving the dull distant landscape a feeling of motion.

How strange—he expected to see the street lined with palm trees. This wasn't your typical suburban southern California Spanish style bungalow with stucco exterior, reddish-orange tile roof and arched portal. The landscape was desert sand and white gravel divided into diamond sections with sporadic desert type plants, cactus and succulents. An ess-shaped sidewalk composed of large pieces of broken ceramic tile curved its way from the end of the lane to the front door. A set of longhorns was nailed over the door. As he approached the front, it occurred to him that as hot as it was outdoors, it looked like it had to be hotter inside this sheet metal box.

Soon after Steve had entered the university, his father came solo to California and somehow ended up in this lonely trailer off the main road. His mother remained in Richburg and continued to run the hardware store. Shortly thereafter, they began divorce proceedings and divided their marital assets, which included their house and business as well as some stock certificates, and insurance policies that they had saved together throughout the years.

He took a part-time job in nearby Cathedral City at Home Depot and remarried. Henry Bolingbroke died of a sudden heart attack and she remained unmarried. Even though his parents' divorce was final and his father had remarried, they continued to battle over a few residual matters that remained unresolved. Steve hadn't spoken to his either of his parents since he had left for university and he had never met Molly, his father's second wife.

After returning from Iraq, Steve obtained his father's address and phone number from his brother and was surprised to learn that his dad was living there in the desert. It seemed somehow that fate was bringing them together, yet at the same time throwing obstacles in the way of their reunion.

At last, unencumbered, he was able to make the phone call. Molly answered and indicated that his father was unable to come to the phone. She didn't say why.

Steve told her that he wanted to drive down to Cathedral City and pay a visit to both her and his father and she indicated that they were usually there and that that would be fine. She seemed eager to meet him. Steve confirmed with her that he would be there within the next two or three days, and he gave her his phone number at the deli in the event any problems arose.

Steve stepped from his truck, slammed the door closed and walked around the front of his pickup. He could feel the heat radiating from the Ford engine, all hundred and fifty horses having worked up a lather.

As he stepped onto the desert floor and regarded the tin box that his father now called home, he thought about how all this was so unlike his dad. Before coming to this wasteland, he had imagined his dad answering the door looking like Hugh Hefner, donning a smoking jacket, a pipe clutched between his teeth, a twenty-two-year-old blond Molly hanging on his shoulder wearing a slinky low-cut evening gown. But then as he approached the front porch, he pictured how he last re-membered him, not the Wizard of the Playboy Mansion, but the proprietor of a small town hardware store, dressed in wool pants, plaid shirt and a gray cardigan sweater with a tape mea-sure clipped to his belt. He saw him teaching his Sunday school class, mowing the lawn, trimming the hedge, reading the news-paper with his feet up on the ottoman and eating breakfast before going to work. He saw him putting his false teeth into a glass before going to bed. Steve saw him running alongside the first time he had ridden a bicycle. He saw him running along pulling a kite up into the air and he saw him shifting gears in the old Chevy. He saw him sick in bed with a ther-mometer in his mouth. He could hear him saying grace before each meal and he saw him driving him in the rain to school. Stepping up to the front door, he remembered the cuckold he hated.

Steve rapped on the screen door: *Rap, rap, rap!* The aluminum door didn't quite fit properly or didn't close cor-rectly and so each time he rapped, it banged against the door-stop and sprang back causing the spring to rattle.

After rapping, he stepped back, and waited—no response. One more time and then he waited; a third time—again, no answer. In addition, each time he rapped, the door banged and sprang back and the spring rattled. It caused a slight echo: *RAP, RAP, RAP, rap, rap, rap, rattle.* He thought he heard a dog barking, coming from inside the house: "Arf, arf, arf, howl,

howl." Then the door started to move inward, a click, and then an air sucking sound as the door slowly pivoted on its axis nearly ninety degrees.

He could feel his heart pounding up one notch from normal as he saw a middle-aged woman that could never have been anyone's mom standing there pushing the screen door outward. She wore a printed blouse and short shorts with an apron around her thin waist that was beginning to show a little spare tire; her hair, blond, straight and teased, not at all like his mother's. Even in her bare feet standing at the door, she appeared to tower over him. Steve made every attempt not to stare at her golden breasts that shook like helium-filled loaves of bread when she moved, that lunged forward like two F-116 fighter jets when she stood still. Her face changed from surprise to a bright smile as she spoke warmly, "Why, you must be Steven! I'm Molly—do come in. Your father is so excited waiting for you to arrive."

Steve smiled, and offered his hand and then quickly withdrew it since she was occupied holding the door opened. "Yes, I'm Steven, your husband's son." He immediately felt embarrassed for having bad timing in offering his hand and for having addressed their marital status.

She wasn't young and she wasn't old, either—just like Lacey, he thought as he placed his right foot over the threshold, she moving back as he penetrated the living room. Actually, she could have looked a little like his mother, except for her height, build, her bronze tan and auburn hair. This was Southern California; maybe he had seen her before in the movies, or in a girlie magazine.

"You look very much like your dad, Steven," she remarked as she closed the front door and headed toward the center of the room. "Especially your bright red hair," she continued. "His isn't so bright anymore and probably a little grayer than when you last saw him, I suspect."

Steve followed her in and quickly scanned the room as he walked. It appeared small, but not cramped, comfortable, with a couch against the front window, a rectangular shaped coffee table and an easy chair with ottoman on line with the small TV at the opposite end of the room. Two fans at opposite ends of the room played air ping-pong. There were the usual knick-knacks scattered about the room, pictures of her relatives and his dad's sister and a protestant image of Christ hanging on one of the walls.

His dad rolled into the room riding a wheel chair, his hands on the large wheels propelling him forward. Attached to his nose was a clear plastic tube that was connected at the other end to a small oxygen tank affixed to the rear of his conveyance. "Hello, Steven," he spoke warmly still rolling forward toward Steve. "It's been a long time, son, and I've missed you."

Steve turned toward his father, stunned at his unexpected appearance. "Hello, Dad. It sure has been a long time," moving toward him and offering his hand.

The two shook hands, his father using both hands, which gave Steve a warm feeling. He took the couch while Molly went to the kitchen to bring in some lemonade and cookies. His dad moved himself into position next to the chair with the ottoman. It seemed as though he was vicariously in that chair. For a moment, no one spoke, the two staring at each other not knowing what to say.

"It sure has been a long time, hasn't it?" Steve repeated. Then he caught himself and said, "I guess I already said that. Dad, tell me about what's going on in your life, the wheel chair, the oxygen tank? I had no idea."

"Cancer, lung cancer," he wheezed as if he had just taken a drag on a helium balloon then spoke slowly catching his breath. "I suppose that you can tell that I'm dying. The doctors went in, looked, and closed me back up and said, 'Sayonara, there's nothing we can do for you, just give you something for the pain.' However, I have to tell you that I'm ready. I've had a good life and I'm all right with the Lord. I just needed to see you one last time and see if we couldn't work things out. I've always been proud of you, son. I haven't shown it. I take that back, I've often shown it, my displeasure that is. I know it and I regret it."

Molly returned from the kitchen with their afternoon snack and sat the tray on the coffee table after serving the two Stevens. She injected into the conversation, "Thomas, your brother, is coming this weekend. I do hope that you'll be able to stay, that way you can all be together."

"Yes, Molly, I'll stay as long as the both of you will have me," turning and looking at his father. Returning toward Molly he asked, "Molly, tell me about you. I know nothing about you."

"Well, my father was a Presbyterian minister and spent my early childhood on the mission field with my parents, in Seoul, Korea. Later, I graduated from college in Pomona and became a teacher, an art teacher and I rotated among the various schools in the school district. Usually most art classes are only one hour, one day a week—not a very high priority, you see. I married a fine young man, a druggist, and we had two children, a boy, Wallace, and a girl, Kristen. They're about your age, a little younger, perhaps. My husband passed away, and I was left alone when I met your father; it was in church. We were both attending Wednesday morning prayer breakfast; we were both in the same group. Well, we married and bought this trailer and here we are now."

Molly was a real mover and a shaker. She was good at conversation and she was quick to help anyone pull his foot out of his mouth if he were so inclined to do so. She was also good at initiating what to do next.

"I have an idea," she said while standing up and smiling at both Stevens. "It's still early enough, not too late that is, why don't you two go for a walk? There's plenty of desert and Steven, you might push him up the lane, turn north and there's a little strip mall there. You might even get a cup of coffee or something. That way you two can get used to each other again. Don't mind me; I've got plenty to do around here."

Molly walked to the front door, opened it and held the screen wide waiting for Steve to push his father out onto the steps. As he brushed near he caught a hint of Desert Bloom and wondered if she always wore it, or just today, or on special occasions. As they arrived at the spot where she was standing, she reached into the pocket on the rear of his chair, pulled out a rumpled angler's hat, and placed in on her husband's head. "That sun is hot out there today, even this late in the afternoon. Oh, it's easier if you take him down the step backwards," she instructed still holding the screen open.

Steve eased him down onto the porch and then one more step down to the desert floor.

"Now you two have a good time, and Steven, don't you let Steven do all the talking!" and she laughed having made a joke and then she closed both doors.

As the two wheeled down the lane and onto the Calle del Las Palmeras, an oncoming car pulled to a stop next to where they were walking. The woman that was driving rolled down the window and called out, "Hello Mr. Franks, how are you feeling today?"

He returned the wave, and answered, "Just fine, Cindy. My son from up north is here to visit. This is Steven, Jr."

Cindy climbed out of her car, closed the door and walked across the sand covered asphalt to where they had stopped and introduced herself, "Hi, I'm Cindy Walker, I live down the road a ways, with my husband. We've known your dad and Molly ever since they moved here. They're both so nice, and that Molly, whatever would we do without her; hey Mr. Franks, isn't that so?"

He smiled and agreed by nodding his head. Then he gasped a little for air and tried to speak; his voice was graveled and he wheezed. "She's wonderful; the love of my life."

The two, father and son, worked their way along the road, bouncing over cracked concrete, around obstacles such as a tricycle that had been left abandoned by some tyke and a parked car along the way.

They shared conversation, Steve about Iraq and his adventures afterward, his girlfriend Moon; his dad about moving to California, meeting Molly and his place in the Presbyterian Church in Cathedral City. His father was a little concerned about what kind of parents would name their daughter Moon. Steve rightly omitted a lot of the detail, including the portion about her ears.

"Well then, do you think that you might marry her? His father spoke while twisting his head slightly to the left and cocking his eyes to an extreme position. After a few seconds with no response he returned his head forward, a little irritated that he hadn't got an answer, and remarked, "I guess that means that you don't know."

Steve didn't respond. They continued along together reaching the strip center that Molly spoke of where there was a small convenience store. He pulled up to the front door, put on the brake lock, walked around to where he could see his father and asked, "Do you still like Drumsticks?"

"Yes, I do, though I haven't had one in a long time."

"OK. You wait here and I'll see if I can get one or two. Do you want to go in or stay out here?"

"I'll just wait here in the shade, you go on in."

Shortly thereafter, Steve returned with two Klondike bars; the store was out of Drumsticks. The ice cream bars, which had always been a favorite of them both, were a perfect substitute. Steve handed one to his dad, began peeling back the aluminum foil wrapper and took a bite. He then sat down on the curb alongside the sidewalk, next to his dad's wheelchair.

His dad was slower getting his unwrapped, but he eventually managed. A big chunk of chocolate coating sprang loose as he took his first bite and he quickly picked it up and stuck it into his mouth with his other hand. As soon as he swallowed his first bite, he paused, and reflected, "Steve, do you remember when you were a little boy and we, I, you, your brother and your mother would go to town on Saturday nights? I'd buy four of these Klondike bars from the Isleys Store and we'd all sit there in the car and eat them. One of us would always get chocolate on something. It's impossible to eat these things without having an accident." He continued to bite into his ice cream while talking. "They're always vanilla now; it used to be that if you opened yours and it was strawberry flavor, then the store manager gave you a second one for free. You don't see that anymore. I still always look though, just in case."

"No, I had forgotten all about that. However, I do remember the time we went fishing up in Michigan; it was up past Sault Ste. Marie. We went trolling for pike. On the way home, you were picked up for speeding through this small town and didn't have enough money to pay the speeding ticket. I was so afraid they were going to put you in jail. Hey! I think I had better get us home or Molly is going to be worried. I don't want her mad at me on the first day."

The next few days went along smoothly. They talked, played cards, went for walks and on Sunday morning they all went to church together at the Cathedral City Presbyterian Church.

Steve helped Molly one morning pull weeds in the garden and then for dinner that night he wanted to fix his specialty—tuna casserole. It was only a can of tuna mixed together with noodles and a can of Campbell's Cream of Mushroom soup, but it tasted good and they all enjoyed it.

Later that night his father asked about his mother, had he seen her or talked to her? He wanted to know how she was doing. Steve replied that he hadn't; he wasn't sure if he would ever see her again.

"I think we should talk about that," his father remarked.

"Why do you say that? It's over; there's nothing left to talk about," Steve replied.

"Steve, try and listen to what I'm about to say. It runs contrary to what you believe, but please, hear me out. On that night when you saw your mother with another man in the car, that was an empty car sitting alongside the road. Now I don't doubt that you believed that you saw something. I'm not convinced that you actually saw what you thought you saw." He paused several times to catch his breath. "That road was on the way to your grandmother's farm and your mother was headed there when her car ran out of gas. She left her car parked there and walked the remaining two miles to the farm. You can check with your grandmother; she will verify thatyour grandfather drove your mother back to her car with a can of gas from their tank there at the farm."

Steve paused, thought, and then spoke. "Why am I just hearing this story now, years later? Why didn't someone tell me before now? If this is true then why did the two of you divorce? It makes no sense to me. I'm sorry, your story is too little too late."

"We all made mistakes and we have all paid dearly for them. To begin with, the rumors that you referred to did in fact exist, but they were unfounded. Your mother and I had become friends with Henry and Maxine Bolingbroke and we were spending a lot of time together. Henry would stop by the store while your mother was there and people began to talk, idle gossip. That isn't your fault. I'm sure you tried not to believe it, but it created a framework for believability. When you came to me with your accusations, I went immediately to your mother who promptly denied that anything had happened. Rather than defending herself by offering an explanation, she felt insulted and refused to participate in what she referred to as your simple-minded insinuations. She demanded my support in getting you to retract your charges. That was wrong. I should never have joined in with her and she should have offered an explanation."

Steve's voice grew louder. "You both tore into me without an explanation; what then was my mistake?"

"Your mistake was merely that you had misconstrued what you believed to be your mother's guilt. It wasn't intentional, but it was a mistake just the same."

"If this is what you believe, then why did you divorce?"

"That's a good question. There was never any issue of infidelity. We'd been drifting apart for sometime and we stayed together until you boys were gone and no longer needed your parents. I wanted to retire and do some traveling; your mother wanted to stay and continue to run the business. She never liked to travel."

Steve began to feel a tightness in his chest; his heart was pounding. Soon he could feel his entire chest, stomach and throat throbbing and he excused himself and went to the bathroom. He locked the door and climbed up on the counter resting his feet in the sink and then sank his fingers into his hair beginning at his forehead, his fingers spread apart, pressing hard against his scalp until his fingertips came together in the back of his head, then holding them there for a moment or two while pressing in on his temples with the palms of his hands. His jaws clenched tightly, repeatedly he drove his hands over and through the top of his head sometimes pulling at his hair as if to rip them from his scalp, each time stopping to press his hand against his temples until he stopped and leaned his face against the mirror. He began to sob and the salty tears wormed their way downward, detouring around the place where the right side of his face pressed against the glass, down to the low point on his chin where they dropped to his shirt below. He then twisted his body and head and pushed the front of his face against the mirror, pressing his forehead, nose, chin and hands onto the glass as if looking through a car window, struggling to make clear the fuzzy image of his mother's car that began to appear.

He pressed one eye flat against the surface as if to get a better glimpse, but the image remained distorted. It certainly was his mother's car that he saw, a beige Belair, but it was impossible to tell who was in it, if anyone. Then in the distance, far to the front of her car he spotted a pair of headlight beams moving slowly toward him along the gravel road eventually stopping directly in front of the parked car on the same side of the road. The bright lights blinded Steven temporarily and he had to turn away. His eyes soon adjusted to the glare and he was then able to see an older man, dressed in OshKosh B'Gosh bib overalls, climb out of the driver's side and take a gas can out of the trunk. It was his grandfather; he was sure of it. He had suffered from phlebitis for several years and had acquired a certain limp that could only be his. His mother emerged from the passenger side of his grandfather's car and she carefully crossed the road in her high-healed shoes, tiptoeing over the gravel toward Steven until they were both almost face to face, her visage several inches above his. She was dressed in an expensive looking camel coat that hung below her knees halfway down her shin, opened at the top revealing a white silk blouse and a red scarf. She wore a small hat perched on the side of her head held in place by a pearl pin. She reached into her purse, pulled out a hanky, and began to wipe the dirt from her side of the mirror and then stooped down, slightly, to look in. She began to speak, "There, my son, can you see more clearly now? Does this straighten out your nasty mind?"

When his grandfather had finished pouring the can of gas, he climbed inside the Belair to see if it would start, and it did. He motioned for her that it was ready and she quickly crossed the road to her car and climbed inside on the passenger side. Almost immediately then, a third vehicle, a powder blue Buick, approached from the opposite direction, bearing down at a high rate of speed, its windows down, its radio blaring and its teenage passengers' heads all bobbing out the four Buick windows looking to see what was going on. As it came along side of the Belair, one of the voices could be heard saying, "Isn't that your mom's car?"

The sleek Buick soon sped away, its tires spinning, throwing stones and gravel behind causing a cloud of gray dust to remain in the air for several minutes to come. His grandfather returned to his car, his mother slid over behind the steering wheel and both vehicles disappeared into the starry night. Steven's face and hands slid down the mirror, making a screeching sound, onto the counter as he heard a rap on the bathroom door, "Steven, are you in there?" It was Molly's voice.

"Yes," he responded, barely audible.

"You've been in there a long time. I just wanted to make sure everything is alright."

Steve waited and then replied, "Everything is OK; I'll be right out."

He waited for a while, climbed down from the counter, slowly opened the door and peered out making sure everyone had gone to bed and he quietly crept down the hallway to his room where he entered without turning on the light, undressed down to his underwear and crawled into bed. Lying on his back, he could see the moon outside. It reflected brightly, high in the northern sky. Reaching down to the floor, he pulled his medallion, the rabbit in the moon, from his pant's pocket and tucked it under his pillow.

Steve's younger brother Thomas lived in Denver, was married and had a baby daughter. They were three years apart and while they were children living at home, their ages were close enough to share some things together, like mealtimes and going to church, and far enough apart to have separate friends and interests.

They both had newspaper routes; Steve's was in the afternoon whereas Thomas' was first thing every morning. After high school they went to separate universities and lived in different parts of the country. They rarely got together and never talked to each other on the phone. Steve had no idea if his brother had been aware of the rumors that had been spread about town and he wasn't going to ask.

Thomas arrived at the front door the following day from Denver. Molly introduced herself and led him in where Steve and his dad were watching a baseball game on the television, Cubs versus the Dodgers, in LA, 1 to 5 in favor of Los Angeles, darn!

Steve looked toward the door and seeing his brother for the first time in several years cried out while jumping up from his seat, "Thomas! Longtime, no see," rushing toward him with his hand outstretched, for a handshake, which turned into a warm embrace.

"Steve, it sure has been. How are you, older brother, war hero? Let's see, you still have both arms, legs, and I suppose everything is functioning all right. You didn't bring back any of those camel spiders with you, did you; no post traumatic stress syndrome or flashbacks, I hope?"

"No, but I did see lots of them; ugly critters they are. So how have you been? You didn't bring Kathy and Debbie with you? I'll bet Debbie has really grown by now, almost ready to start school?"

"They're both fine; Debbie starts kindergarten next year."

By this time Thomas had seen his Dad slouched in his easy chair, his head poked forward, watching his two sons with vivid interest, a clear plastic tube hanging from his nostrils to the canister of oxygen at the side of his chair. Thomas walked toward him as he struggled to climb out of his chair and Thomas took hold of his arm and steadied him as he got control of his balance.

"Hello, Dad. You've always kept too many secrets! I wish I'd known sooner."

"Don't worry, I'm just fine. I'm sixty-seven years old this past July and I've had a wonderful life. I'm happy now that my two boys are here with me, and Molly, my sweet wonderful Molly. You've met her, haven't you?"

"Yes, Dad, just now. She's a real looker. Just how do you rate?"

"Well, the Lord has always taken good care of me—thank you, Jesus. I suppose he sent her for that purpose. Where is she now? Molly where are you? I want to share you with my boys; I want us all to be together. Honest, I'm just feeling great!"

The next few days were filled with joyous celebration, laughing and storytelling of their earlier years. They took several trips pushing their dad to the strip mall where they exhausted the supply of Klondike bars and began working on the Creamsicles.

"Ok, boys, I've a question for you both. What's the difference between a Creamsicle and a Dreamsicle?"

Steve thought he knew the answer. "That's easy; they're both the same, just different names, different companies."

"No, that isn't the correct answer. How about you Thomas; any idea?"

"Sorry, Dad, I don't know."

"Well, you two bright college boys can't answer a simple question like that? The sherbet-like shell of the Creamsicle is identical to that of the Dreamsicle, but the payoff inside is ice cream in the former, ice milk in the latter. The difference in price, last time I checked, was about a nickel."

Steven, Thomas and their father sat in front of the television watching a football game. It was the opening game of the season, fourth quarter and Miami was leading Pittsburg 17-14. Pittsburg had moved the ball all the way down the field to the one-yard line, fumbled and turned the ball over to Miami. Miami moved it back down the field to their end and were then forced to make a fourth down punt giving the ball back to Pittsburg. Pittsburg then surprised everyone by running eighty-seven yards with the ball and crossing the goal line, putting Pittsburg ahead, 20-17. The Miami coach threw out a red flag challenging the touchdown with the hope that a replay would show that the runner had stepped outside the sideline immediately before scoring. However, the referee failed to see the flag and Pittsburg successfully scored the extra point winning the game 21-17. The Miami coach was outraged. Actual replay of the goal clearly showed that the runner had stepped out-of-bounds and that the Miami coach had in fact tossed in the red flag prior to the point conversion kick.

When the game was over, the three men went outside, and cooked hamburgers over the charcoal grill, sat the picnic table (their father remained in his wheel chair), drank a few bruskies, and watched the sun settle itself into the desert sand like a yellow cat in the autumn sun. Steven formed the large round patties and watched them sizzle over the red-hot coals. Spikes of flames shot upward through the black grill as drops of grease oozed onto the embers and Steven had to keep turning the burgers to keep them from charring. The hot, arid desert day unable to retain its warmth became the cool desert night and Molly brought an afghan to the aging patriarch. As the door slammed behind her, the lizards ran.. A light breeze began to stir the smoke coming from the grill sending it into Steven's face. He liked the smell of things burning outside— especially burgers or sausages over a grill or freshly raked leaves burning in the autumn. He began to tear, not from the smoke, but from the onions that he was slicing on the small ledge at the side of the grill. Through the smoke, he could see the moon in the northeastern sky and then off, further east, he could see Orion and its belt, home to one of the most beautiful objects in the night sky, the Orion Nebula. The third "star" down in Orion's sword is not a star at all, but the Orion nebula.

Thomas sat at the picnic table; his mind was still on the afternoon game. He was able to relate a similar incident that had occurred once at a Denver Bronco game. "I went home that day feeling cheated," he said. "The stats show that we lost that game," he continued, "but, we really did win, regardless, at least in my mind, that is."

"I guess it's only one's perception that counts," Steven chimed in.

A distant coyote echoed the thought. So did a Mexican free-tailed   bat.

Even though their father had to remain in a wheelchair connected to his oxygen tank and he tired easily, they went one day to the Living Desert Zoo & Gardens, a conservation center for desert plants and animals, and the next to the Palm Spring Aerial Tramway and rode to the top of the San Jacinto Mountains. Molly made sandwiches and they took along a cooler with a six-pack of beer.

After a week or so, Thomas returned to Denver; Steve remained for one additional week and then left for Big Sur.

Two weeks later, Molly called to let him know that his father had passed away. He had taken a turn for the worse; Molly had no longer been able to care for him and he had entered a local hospice, a place for terminally ill patients where treatment focused on the patient's well-being rather than a cure. Molly had been present when he died.

Richburg, Indiana

It was a cold day
The sky was gray
And snow began to fall.

It appeared to Steve that so many things were happening all at once. No sooner had he reconciled with his father, his father died. He would be buried at their home in Richburg and Steve had decided to attend the funeral. That would give him an opportunity to visit his mother and attempt to restore their relationship. And if all that weren't enough, Moon was pregnant, and they hadn't yet discussed what they were going to do.

She had told him the day before he left for Cathedral City, and he thought about it on and off while away visiting with his brother and dad. It was difficult for him to forget about Trudy much the same as it wasn't easy for Moon to forget Jordan. His seeing Trudy on the beach the first afternoon that she arrived at Big Sur, and then later at Captain Bob's wedding, hadn't helped any either. She had never looked more beautiful. But Trudy wasn't pregnant; Moon was, and he was the father.

He wondered how he could remain in Big Sur and earn a living. There was nothing there for him to do other than waiting tables at the deli. He thought about the possibility of opening a store, a gift shop, maybe, and selling souvenirs; but that idea really didn't interest him that much.

Steve was always willing to do the right thing, even if there were a price to be paid in doing it. That is how he found himself in that Hum-V in Kirkuk flying through the air among body parts of one of his fellow soldiers, landing upside down next to a pile of garbage, and awakening in a Mash unit with IVs in his arm and plaster around various parts of his body.

There wasn't much need for further mental debate. He was responsible for getting Moon pregnant, he liked her as much as any woman, maybe even more than most, and if she would have him, he would be glad to marry her.

Steve boarded the small commuter plane at the Monterey-Salinas Airport for a quick one-hour trip to San Francisco. There, he changed planes for a non-stop flight directly to Indianapolis.

It was a warm, west coast day and he had read the weather reports for Indy—cold, snowy and windy. He had no winter clothes so he packed a couple of long-sleeve shirts, a sweatshirt and a windbreaker.

As the 747 pulled away from SFO and soon crossed the Sierra Nevada's, he looked down at the snowcapped peaks and remembered that since he had come to California, he hadn't yet tried his hand, or feet that is, at skiing—one of the things he had wanted to do. (He never seemed to get around to doing many things.) He expected that there was going to be snow when he reached Indiana. He remembered how his mom always made him wear his boots when he walked to school in the snow, something the other kids didn't seem to have to do. Wearing boots, he thought, made him look like a sissy. Once he walked away from the house, stashed them in the neighbor's bushes, and then retrieved them when he returned home. And as you would expect, his shoes were so wet that she knew right away and took a switch to him. Sometimes it seemed that the switch was preferable to being teased. That was so long ago. He realized that if he had a pair of boots now he probably wouldn't feel intimidated in wearing them.

At Indianapolis Airport, he exited the aircraft through the enclosed skywalk to the terminal and sauntered to the car rental kiosk where he picked up the keys to a Dodge Stratus.

The cold sub-zero wind smacked him in the face as he opened the door to the outside parking lot. After a year in Baghdad and then several months in California, he had forgotten the feeling of Midwestern cold, that meat-locker cold that made the moisture in his nostrils turn to ice. Wearing only a light windbreaker he cursed the cold as he ran to the stall where his car was parked slipping on the icy pavement along the way.

As he approached the car, he struggled to keep his arms and body from shaking as he fumbled for the keys in his pocket. His shivering caused him difficulty in inserting the key in the door lock and then in the ignition, but at least once the door was closed he finally escaped the cold wind.

The route to Richburg usually took about an hour. The first half of the way was on the interstate and the balance was on Country Road 37, which carved its way through fallow fields where stubs of dead cornstalks protruded through the crusty layers of snow.

The trees growing along the fencerows between the fields had lost their leaves weeks earlier and now appeared lifeless, even a bit scary, like monsters prowling, tramping and waving their gnarly moss-covered fingers in the cold wind.

As the Dodge Stratus cruised along, sliding occasionally on the slippery patches of ice, past the weather-beaten farmhouses and barns along the way, what little color remained in the afternoon grayness crawled into a foxhole to take cover for the night. Living room lights shining through their frost covered windows bore witness that there was yet life in this desolate countryside.

At last, he reached the town limits, where the sign read, 'Welcome to Richburg, Home of the Cougars'. The pavement changed from asphalt to brick and the hum of the tires changed to a loud shaking like having just put a quarter in the vibrating bed in a low-priced motel. He eased his foot on the break pedal until the speedometer read thirty-five, the posted limit, and then coasted into the center of town.

He stopped for two red lights before continuing on to the outskirts, on the other side of town, where his mother still lived in the family home. As he pulled into the snow-covered driveway, he saw a single dim light in the living room and parked the Stratus. The back door was locked, and there was a note taped to the window which read:

'We are at Ballanger's Funeral Home.'

Steve went there directly. As he walked in the front door, he was greeted by friends and relatives, all people that he had known as a child. His aunts, uncles, cousins, and women from the church, all were there. There were storeowners and shop-keepers from the drug store, the Dairy Queen and the furniture store as well as the butcher, the baker and candlestick maker. There were classmates from his high school and there was Trudy.

She approached him solemnly and offered a hug that he received. She offered her condolences and he thanked her as he moved beyond, toward the casket. Off to the side he could see his brother and mother sitting together, and as he approached, his brother rose and greeted him. It had only been a couple of weeks ago that he had seen him in Cathedral City— although not well, his dad had still been very much alive then.

"It's good to see you again, Thomas," he spoke as they exchanged hugs. He looked down and saw his mother, who was wiping tears from her face with a small embroidered hanky. She hadn't seen or recognized him. Steve didn't know that his mother's eyesight was failing.

Then she turned toward him and asked, "Is that you, Steven? Do I hear your voice?"

Steve moved directly in front of her, reached for her thin pale hand, and answered, "Yes, mother, it's me."

She immediately rose from her chair and looked at him directly and spoke, "I thought that I heard you when you came in; I wasn't sure. Did you go to the house?"

"Yes, I stopped there first and saw the note."

As he looked at her, he could see how she had aged. She was much thinner and her wig was on crooked. Her makeup, her rouge and lipstick, had been applied unevenly and she was no longer able to stand straight.

"How nice you look," he lied. "It's been so long since I've been home."

"Yes, that's right." She spoke while still holding his hand. "Your dad had to die to get you here! Come sit down with me. Tell me what all you've been up to."

"Mom, we can talk later? Right now I want to go to my father's casket."

"Yes, son, we'll talk later."

Steve moved to the edge of his father's gray, felt-covered pine box. It was a simple inexpensive casket. It was how his father wanted it. He studied his face. It would be the last time. It was full of color and his hair was neatly combed. His eyes were closed as if he were asleep. He had been dressed in a white shirt and sharp blue pinstriped suit with vest and red tie. On his right hand, he wore his Mason's ring, 32nd degree of the Ancient and Accepted Scottish Rite of Freemasonry, and on his left, his wedding band.

"Wake up, Daddy, wake up! Please, come on. He's been here. I just checked. He ate one of the cookies and drank all of the milk that we left out for him. Please, Daddy, wake up, it's Christmas."

"OK, OK, get your brother and I'll be right down." He slowly ambled into the shower.

"Hurry, Daddy! Are you still sleeping? Are you up yet? Daddy, I just peeked and Santa left a bicycle under the tree. Do you think it's for me or for Thomas? Please! I can't stand waiting any longer. Please wake up, please."

His childhood and his relationship with his father had been a mix of love and hate. Now all the hate had died along with his father, all he could think of now was how much he loved his father. Even in his strictness, there was love; he was a man of integrity, of principal.

"Daddy, let's go swimming. We could go for a picnic. I'd be glad to make peanut butter and jelly sandwiches; and we could roast marshmallows."

One of the women from the church appeared and spoke to Steve, "He was a wonderful man, humble and he walked with God."

"Daddy; could you help me put this worm on the hook? It keeps slipping off."

"Thank you, Mrs. Drake, we will all miss him." Steve responded and walked back to his mother and brother.

When everyone had left, Steve, Thomas and their mother all returned to the family home where other family members and friends had already gathered. They had come with salads, casseroles, and an assortment of breads, lunchmeats and desserts. The guests hung on several hours after his mother had gone to bed. Thomas and Steven really didn't feel like visiting, but remained cordial and pleasant until the last of the guests had departed.

The funeral was scheduled for the following morning at Saint Andrew's Episcopal Church. Then afterwards he would be taken to the cemetery where a short eulogium would be delivered before he would be lowered into the frozen Indiana earth. The adjacent empty plot remained silently asleep waiting for the day when it too would awaken, spread wide its jowls and receive his mother to digest her remains, returning ashes to ashes and dust to dust, a ritual repeated over and over since the first Adam was laid to rest.

The next morning Steve was awakened by a knock at the door. It was Trudy. The warm eastern sun shown though her hair, and he stood captivated by her charming country manner. She had an air of lightness and a blue bow in her long blond pageboy. She wore a blue plaid jumper cut a few inches above her knee-high socks that added to her girlish appeal. As he stood staring, he saw a robin alight onto a nearby fence. *How strange,* he thought, *it's not yet spring.*

"I can't stay," she said, "I just came over to bring this apple pie that I baked this morning. Oh, how foolish of me! I guess you have plenty of these sorts of things already, don't you?"

Steve stepped back from the door and invited her in. She handed him the pie and he took it to the kitchen, returned and led her into the living room that was off the entry. "Please sit down, Trudy."

After an exchange of compliments and small talk, Steve blurted it out. "Moon and I have decided to marry." A long cold silence followed as if they had been encased in a giant ice cube, the two of them looking at each other through its cool blue hue. Slowly, the ice began to thaw. "We're going to have a baby." The only thing left of the ice cube now was a puddle of water and it had just soaked into the carpet.

Trudy was seemingly able to control her emotions and only mildly expressed her disappointment. "I had always hoped that some day the two of us…" Then she began to cry as she reached for a tissue in her jumper pocket, her visage slightly flushed "I'm sorry to be like this. You must forgive me for not being more enthusiastic, congratulatory. But, you see, I was sure that somehow you come back, like always before, and then when the time was right, it would be the two of us having that baby."

Steve felt the urge to go to her and comfort her, but resisted. Instead, he offered only a hasty excuse. "I'm not sure how things got this far with Moon, but they did. After all, aren't you and Fred getting married?"

"Oh, Fred? Yes, I suppose so. Actually, no—I never really intended to—you know how it is? We drift into these situations; they look good for a moment, and then the next day they look different. Like, have you written a letter to someone, full of emotion and feeling, only to read it the next morning and tear it up?"

Steve nodded, quietly as the two of them rose from their seats and headed for the entry. As he opened the door, she turned and the two embraced and kissed. He felt the wetness of her tongue and notice how quickly he had become aroused, his heart pounding, bolts of energy zigzagging throughout his body, he, realizing for the first time in his life that he loved her and that he was about to lose her. Quietly, he released her and walked with her to her car in the driveway, neither of their feet touching the ground. As she pulled away, he thought he could see her running though the cornfield, in the back of the house on the way to the lake; he was running beside her—they had been swimming there, once, skinny dipping—she could run almost as fast as he.

As he turned around and started toward the house, he stopped and remembered the day that she saw him off to Iraq.

"I'll be back soon, this war won't last long, I promise."

"I'm so afraid for you, darling, you'll be careful, won't you?"

[182]

"Yes, we have the best army in the world."

"Write to me, please."

He never wrote or answered any of her letters; it hadn't seemed important, at the time. She was always there, when he needed a date or was lonely. He wanted her now, but now, things had changed; there was Fred, Moon and a baby.

As Steve closed the door and walked slowly into the kitchen, he was dripping with perspiration. His mother came down the stairs from her upstairs bedroom. "Was someone here?" she asked. "I thought that I heard talking."

"It was Trudy, she brought us a pie," he answered while wiping his face with a hand towel. "I put it in the kitchen."

"Oh, that's too bad. I would like to have seen her. How is she, anyway?"

"She's fine. I think that she's getting married. I met the guy in California, Fred Saladburger's his name—nice guy."

"Oh, that's too bad. I would have liked the two of you to have married. She always seemed perfect for you. Do you have a girlfriend, yet?"

"Actually, yes, I do. In California, her name is Moon."

"Moon? What kind of name is that? Is she one of those California hippies?"

"Now, Mom, you shouldn't talk that way; you don't even know her."

"Well, then, why didn't you bring her home, introduce her, show her off?"

"It didn't seem like the right time. After all, you and I, we haven't spoken for some time now, and with the funeral."

He paused and then told her, "We're getting married."

"Married? In addition, you have never introduced her! Well can you tell me when this is going to take place, and where, and am I invited?"

"It just happened, I mean we just decided. Then dad passed away and we weren't able to get it together. I caught the first plane and came home, and now I'm telling you. No one else knows, except Trudy, that is, who I just told a few minutes ago."

The elevated voices reached the upstairs bedroom where Thomas was awakened and made it down the stairs and into the living room, where Steve was explaining to his mother. Actually, the turn of events were quite convenient as the funeral and then the surprise wedding announcement all created a working scenario that brought the family together again without having to confront the issue that had torn them apart. As they sat together in the living room, it was if the past was over and they were now participating in the present. The family was now reunited and they spent the remaining part of the day, a mother with her two sons, together.

That evening they drove to neighboring Delaware and had sandwiches at a Subway restaurant. The following day Thomas returned to Denver and Steve to Big Sur.

The Wedding

The great day of the wedding had finally arrived. Starr and Sirius were both scrambling to put together the last-minute touches. Both Steve's mother and stepmother had arrived from Richburg and Cathedral City the day before and shared the last remaining bedroom of the Light house. The grounds at the deli had been decorated with ribbons, balloons, and banners containing well-wishes for the couple. This included the parking lot in front as well as the inside of the deli, the veranda and the upper level of the land in the rear. Below on the beach they had erected several tents with multi-colored banners flying in the breeze at each mast top. On the veranda, several long banquet tables replaced the small round coffee tables that usually occupied that spot. The tables were decorated with white tablecloths, several bouquets of wild flowers and small statues of angels and cherubs.

The wedding dais was a platform rented from A-1 Rental in Monterey. It stood on the beach below the rock face, positioned halfway between the surf and the rocky cliff. It was covered with a large Persian rug and decorated with flowers, a white portal and a picket fence. The stage was set up so that after the couple said their vows they would walk through the opening, down the step toward the surf and then back toward the rocks up to the veranda. At the left side of the dais, toward the rocks, there was a tent with chairs for the musicians, who would remain seated as they played the prelude and the wedding march.

Captain Bob and Lacey were the first to arrive. Always a glutton for attention, Bob pulled into the parking lot with his Fisherman's Wharf captain's hat covered head protruding from his metallic-silver Rolls convertible, sans top, horn honking and Lacey waving. He carefully backed the massive vehicle onto two parking spots, as if he were maneuvering an M1A2 Abrams battle tank, somewhat diagonally, assured that he wouldn't receive any door dings on this festive, possibly alcoholic day. Like the roses of Lancaster and York, the Santa Barbarans unfolded—Bob the red, with his gaily colored Hawaiian shirt hanging untucked beneath his blue blazer and Lacey, a white camellia, donning a silk form-fitting blouse and a long loose-knitted skirt, which draped over her flip-flops. Unfortunately, since Steve, Moon, Starr and Sirius were indisposed and none of the other guests had yet arrived, the whole show went unnoticed.

Raol, standing tall, and Ofilia, not so very much, like Latin Mutt and Jeff, were the next to arrive. Her beautiful handcrafted multi-colored serape paled against her beaming white-toothed smile, freckled with bits of gold. His long ears hung beneath his leather porkpie hat almost to his shoulders, speaking of his familial resemblance to the bride.

They entered the empty deli and slowly worked their way back to the veranda where Bob was taking the initiative and uncorking one of the several bottles of Edna Valley Vineyards 'Paragon' submerged in a galvanized tub of ice. Looking up, Bob introduced himself and Lacey and proceeded to pour the buttery chardonnay evenly into four of the assembled plastic champagne glasses that he had removed from the cardboard box beneath the table. Inviting each of them to take a goblet, he raised his to eye level and presented a smiling, "cheers!"

The other guests appeared over the next hour, Trudy and Fred Saladburger, then Havana Charpantier and Addis Abba. To everyone's surprise, Dollfuss Simpson and Jerry Red feather walked in, both with beaming smiles on their faces as if it were Christmas and they had just seen Santa Clause coming down the chimney. Dollfuss and Captain Bob both toasted the end of their dispute and went off to the edge to share a doobie.

The musicians strolled in with their instruments in machinegun cases followed by the Reverend Rita, the cleric hired to officiate the ceremony, who walked in stiff as a Gibson truss rod. The musicians were all dressed in black and white formals, the men with top hats and the women in white low-cut sequined gowns. Reverend Rita was an older woman, in a gray Nero jacket worn over a white turtleneck sweater, whom Starr had met once during a break at a Rolfing class at Eselan.

Moon sat at her dressing table, in her room upstairs in the main house. The window was open and she could hear the commotion and noise of the guests gathering below. Some were talking loudly, joking, laughing. It was obvious that many had already had more than enough chardonnay, this early in the morning. She sat in front of the mirror admiring her nakedness. Her body parts were now becoming round: her significant abdomen, her tiny breasts, her face, and her ears. She enjoyed caressing her tummy, her fingertips making gentle circular motions barely touching her soft skin.

A black and white picture in an ornate pewter frame of Henri Delgado, her father, whom she could barely remember, rested on the dresser top. His hair was flaxen, long and wavy, shoulder length, with thick eyebrows, a moustache and van dyke. He was standing, posing in front of their VW microbus, parked in front of the Country Store Café holding his guitar case with two fingers raised in the shape of a V, the peace sign. She imagined that it was her mother taking the picture and that she and Sirius were inside the bus, only blurred images behind the fogged windows.

In traditional weddings, the father gives the bride away, but in this marriage ceremony, it would be Starr. Moon loved her mother—the only one in her life that she could ever count on—and she would give her to Steven. Her dead father couldn't be trusted any more than Jordan alive.

She had met Jordan at a Friday night school sponsored dance, after a home football game. She had sat alone along the wall until he had asked her to dance—a slow dance—and she had accepted. She had not seen him before that night. He took her hand and she carefully placed her right arm about his waist as she could see the other girls doing. He held her firmly and she followed. She could feel her heart pounding and her palms perspiring and when he asked her name she could only respond, "Moon, Moon Light." Jordan was unsure if she were telling him her name or that she wanted to step outside with him and he presumed the latter.

He led her to the door and out where the smokers were congregating, to a ledge near the front door where they both sat and talked. He seemed very good-looking and he was easy to talk with. They shared stories of their lives, she about having lived with her mother at the deli and being home-schooled and he about his desire to follow his father's footsteps as a veterinarian.

When she returned home, Moon told her mother that she was in love. She had never met anyone like him before, so handsome, so bright, easygoing, a bright future and she could tell, he liked her.

Throughout his remaining two years in high school, they dated. They were together constantly and they did all the things that high school sweethearts do: cruising, movies, dances, football games, pizza, TV, telephone conversations and sex. Jordan knew her story, about her hippy parents, and about her ears and none of that ever seemed to be an issue for him, that is, until it was time for him to graduate.

Moon understood that he would be going to Cal Poly soon, but she didn't know that he would be breaking off their relationship. Starr, like a cobbler's shoeless children was caught unaware. When it happened, Moon was shocked and overcome with heartache. She had been abandoned, first by her father and now by Jordan.

Suddenly, Starr entered the room without knocking, and Moon came out from behind a cloud. "It's almost time to start and you aren't ready! Moon felt embarrassed and quickly arose from her seat and covered herself with a cotton sheet that was at the edge of her bed.

"Mother, you startled me," she spoke as Starr reached for her white gown that was hanging from the ceiling chandelier.

"It's time for you to quit looking at yourself and get dressed. Reverend Rita and all the guests have arrived. Let me help you get dressed."

At last, mother and her princess walked down the stairs together, arm in arm, flowers in their hair and rings on their fingers and toes, each tall and graceful, proud and full of expectation, and joined the many guests who waited patiently for them on the veranda.

The minute hand on all the timepieces in the world stood straight up as if a universal clock drill sergeant had called them to attention. Reverend Rita announced to the musicians and guests that it was time to take their positions to begin the ceremony.

Starr Light and Moon Light proceeded out the side door, through the garden and moved slowly in the direction of the steps leading down to the beach. Rita stepped onto the dais and remained facing the ocean. The guests all formed a semicircle around the stage. The musicians began playing Canon in D as the bridal party formed at the base of the rock face.

The procession began at the sound of Bridal Chorus led by her brother Sirius, followed by the bride and her mother. They tromped barefooted through the deep, loose silica. When Moon realized how clumsy they looked, trying unsuccessfully to be formal, she began laughing and childishly kicking sand with her toes. The guests, seeing the humor in the event began applauding, and the foursome climbed onto the stand as Reverend Rita turned facing them and remained standing silently as if she were waiting for the music to terminate.

The music continued as if it would never end and slowly developed into a mixture of melodies, sounds and percussions blaring loudly and simultaneously, a cacophony of violins, ocarinas and conch shells; Wagner, Hayden and Bach; Canto Ceremonial, Huaranducha campechana, and Santa Lucia; and Paul Stookey, (singing, *There Is Love*) all competing to be heard. Atmospheric electricity relit the darkened sky with bolts of zigzag flashes of light, seconds before the crack and echo of the lagging, but equally impressive, thunder. The sea began to swell; the surf began to rush toward the dais almost touching it, wave following wave, streams of water, rush and thunder, repeatedly charging the wedding party. There was a bright flash and before everyone's eyes, Reverend Rita became transformed, shape shifted into a glamorous diva dressed in white, long hair flowing down her back, blowing in the gale. She began singing the Bridal Chorus from Lohengrin, "Here comes the bride..." As she sang, her dress began changing, shredding into patches of white and black. Her long black hair began curling, electrified into ringlets that became transformed into black and gray serpents dangling about her face, hissing, with long thin tongues darting in and out of their oval shaped heads. She continued to sing. Next, the black and white patches of her dress began peeling off, falling to the ground. At the instant that the black patches reached the sand, they turned into long, legless vipers that snaked along the beach to the surf and out to sea. The white patches became gray stippled doves that flew upward, through the fog, mist and clouds, toward the hidden sun. The spiral curls of her hair then formed into a bird's nest containing a pair of turtledoves. The resting, cooing, spotted fowl remained for a brief moment and then joined the other doves that had once been white patches of the Reverend's dress. Beneath the exterior of falling patches and bird's nest was the wrinkled skin and white hair of an old man looking much like Moses.

At that, the surf suddenly settled and the music stopped. As everyone looked around in disbelief, they noticed that Starr and Sirius were no longer on the dais rather they were standing in the sand with the other guests. On the right side of the stage stood Steve and Trudy and on the left, Moon and Jordan Charnofsky. So stunned were everyone that no one noticed that Moon's ears had returned to normal—also Raol's and his baby boy's.

Then, from the voice of the old Moses man, the shape shifted Reverend Rita, attired in a white robe and a bright multi-colored feathered headdress, standing in front of the two couples—he stood much shorter—came these words, "I have come that your lives may be set straight and to reconcile that which is in your hearts with reality. Moon, with your consent (you always have free will) the baby that you are carrying, from this day on, is the seed of Jordan, who will be your husband at the end of this ceremony. You will notice Jordan that her ears as well as all the long ears in the world have been returned to what most consider as normal. (I still like long ears.) The only exception to this is Starr Light, who has no need of my interference, and she will retain her beautiful long ears. When I gave Quilaztli this gift five centuries ago, I did it because she was special, unique and I had hoped that they would serve her and her generations well. I always felt bad that it didn't go over so well."

Then he began to fade away; Reverend Rita reappeared in his stead and asked, "And who gives away this bride?"

From the audience came the voice of Sirius. "Her mother and I, to Jordan with our love, may they live in peace and prosperity."

With that, Reverend Rita turned to Jordan and Moon and asked them the age old question, "Do you Moon…? Do you Jordan…?"

Looking at each other, smiling and holding hands they both replied, "I do."

Reverend Rita had finished, the ceremony was completed. Moon and Jordan kissed and walked through the portal and off the dais, around the beach, and then up the rock face to the veranda for the celebration.

Epilogue I

When the wedding was over the only remaining unfinished business was that of Trudy, the rabbit. Her leg had finally healed and during the wedding reception, she was seen to be jumping in her cage, wanting out. Moon reached into the pen and withdrew the furry bunny that had spent the last few weeks eating organic yummies from the Big Sur Deli. Moon handed the lagomorph to Steve, who held it in his arms stroking its back and long ears.

Steve and the two Trudys all rode together in the pickup to the site along Highway 1 where he had run over the rabbit on that foggy night. He pulled over to the side of the road at the exact spot, opened the door and sat Trudy, the rabbit, down onto the ground. She quickly ran into the thicket and that was the last that she was seen, except perhaps, on any moonlight night, when the moon is full, if one were to look closely, you could almost make her out.

Steve returned home and he and Trudy were married. Moon and Steve continued to correspond by e-mail, their relationship becoming much like that of a brother and sister.

Epilogue II

Seated at the head of a long table behind a microphone sits Sonnbeam Franks Charnofsky. He is there at the Barns & Noble Book Store in Monterey, California having just completed the delivery of his short address to an audience of literary reporters and public who are anticipating that his lecture will be followed by a book signing.

SFC: "Now that you have heard my story, are there any questions?"

Member of audience: "This is certainly not your family's biography is it? It's too unbelievable."

SFC: "Yes, I expected that there would be questions, so I have brought with me my grandmother, Starr Light."

Starr Light is seated on the right-hand side of Sonnbeam. Her body is erect, poised and comfortable with her hands folded in her lap. She appears as a woman of considerable years with long gray hair streaming down the side of her face, down her front and back several inches below her shoulders. She seems to have the look of one who has acquired the wisdom of the ages. Part of the time, she appears very happy to be there and other times she resembles the last rose of summer. From her neck hangs a gold medallion worn once by the Mayan Princess Omecoatl that bears the image of the rabbit in the moon.

SFC: "Are there any questions for my grandmother?"

Member of audience: "We are all very anxious to see your very famous ears. Mrs. Light, would you please let us see them?"

Starr then stands and pulls her long hair back behind her ears, tying it with a ribbon that she brought with her for that purpose. The room is instantly filled with oohs, auhs, camera clicks and flashes. Like a professional model, she turns first one way and then the other. When it seems that everyone has had their fill of pictures, she returns to her seat.

Member of audience: "Mrs. Light."

Starr: "You may address me as Starr or Starr Light. I prefer either of those appellations over Mrs. Light."

Member of audience: "Thank you, Starr. Now, I was wondering, how did you feel when you realized that everyone else's ears changed mysteriously from being elongated to what many would call normal, everyone but yours? How did you feel about that?"

Starr: "You must understand that I accepted my ears as a divine gift from a higher power. I was proud that I had been born of that royal line. It would have been a great loss to me should they have been taken from me. Therefore, you ask, 'How did I feel?' I felt all the more consecrated and set apart. How sad it must be for one to live one's life ungrateful for his or her uniqueness whether it is a special mark, the color of one's skin or if one would be so fortunate to be born with three arms."

Member of audience: "Sonnbeam, we would like to know what it's like having two fathers. Do you have any preference of one over the other or do you even consider Steve Benet Franks your father?"

SFC: "By the way, I actually have three fathers: two earthly fathers and one heavenly father. The best way I can think of to answer that question is to ask you a question. Between your mother and father, which do you love more?"

Member of audience: "I love them both."

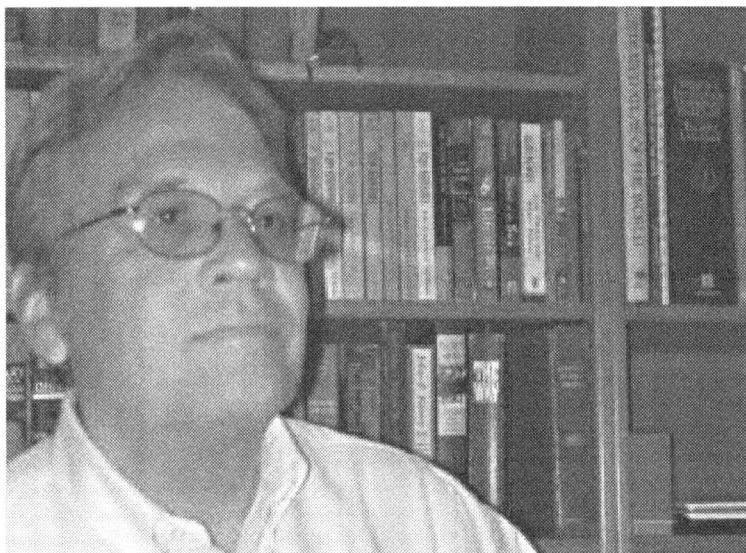

Born in Ohio in 1943, CHARLES GILL came to California while in the army at Fort Ord and has remained there living in the San Franciso and Monterey Bay Areas. After graduating from Ohio State University he served in Viet Nam and has owned and operated an escrow company in Santa Clara, California for 30 years. This is his first novel.